Dark Days in Chicago:

The Rehabilitation of an Urban Street Terrorist

written by:

Adolfo Davis, Stanley Davis, Patrick Pursley

with Larry L. Franklin

HP

History Publishing Media Group LLC

New Castle, Delaware

ISBN 9781940773742

SAN: 850-5942

Published in the United States by
History Publishing, Media Group LLC
New Castle, DE 19720

First Edition

The Authors

Adolfo Davis:

I was arrested at the age of 14 for two counts of first-degree murder, two counts of attempted murder, and home invasion. I was found guilty on all counts and sentenced to life without the possibility of parole. I am now 40 years old, and have spent my life in prison because I allowed my circumstances to turn me into an Urban Street Terrorist. In 2017 I was resentenced to 60 years, allowing me to serve 30 years for good behavior. I will be eligible for parole on December 31, 2020.

Stanley Davis:

At the age of 19, I was arrested for first-degree murder, found guilty, and sentence to 45 to 105 years. After serving over 20 years for another murder, I was once again found guilty and sentenced to life without the possibility of parole. I will never walk the streets again because I had an Urban Street Terrorist state of mind.

Patrick Pursley:

I was a Gangster Disciple on the streets of Chicago; a hustler and petty criminal who has spent most of my life in prison. I am serving life without parole for a crime that I did not commit. My reputation as an Urban Street Terrorist led to my conviction. (Today, in 2017, Pursley is in cook county jail awaiting a new trial.)

Larry L. Franklin, Editor

It has been my honor to assist Adolfo Davis, Patrick Pursley, and Stanley Davis in the completion of their book. While the story is presented in third-person, it was my challenge to give it a cumulative-voice of three, like-minded inmates determined to tell their story. Unless indicated, the words represent the thoughts of Adolfo, Patrick and Stanley.

The authors have spent their incarceration in an Illinois maximum-security prison, while Adolfo spent four of those years in a supermax prison. There were times when the three of them attended prison classes and shared a common goal of writing a book; communicated their ideas while walking in the prison yard and the occasional trips to the gym. Unlike most of us who have our favorite writing spots -- private study, isolated cabin, library, or perhaps a table tucked away in the corner of a coffee shop – the authors wrote their story in a 6 x 9 foot prison cell. Adolfo combined the writings into what would become a manuscript.

It was behind the concrete walls and iron bars of the prison where Adolfo, Patrick, and Stanley sought salvation, as well as giving back to those they have harmed. *Dark Days in Chicago: the rehabilitation of an Urban Street Terrorist* gives testimony to their lives as they remember the freedom they once had. The driving force behind this work was a shared commitment to explain their violent ways, and explore the newfound secrets to a better life. Their desire to help the at-risk youth of Chicago -- the place where street gangs rule – gave Adolfo, Patrick, and Stanley a reason to wake up each morning, a reason to live.

Foreword

There are a special group of forgotten men who live in the Stateville Correctional Center, a maximum-security prison located in Crest Hill, Illinois. Each of them spent their early years as gang members on the streets of Chicago. All three were convicted of first-degree murder and sentenced to life without parole. Each has served over 25 years in an Illinois prison.

The temptation to continue their gang activity while incarcerated was strong. Protection, contraband, money, and the allure of a prison family fulfilled their immediate needs. But amidst the violence and quiet roar of 2,550 troubled inmates, a miracle happened. Three like-minded inmates – Adolfo Davis, Patrick Pursley, and Stanley Davis – sought redemption as well as a need to give back to those they have harmed.

Words give testimony to their lives, thoughts, and concerns as they reflect upon their youth and the freedom they once had. Their intent is to help transform young people on the streets and promote life, not death. These men share the history that steered them towards prison. It is their hope and prayer that this book supports healing, thoughtful reflection, and awareness of the 2.3 million adults and juveniles incarcerated in America's state and federal prisons. An0d for the at-risk youth who are making choices that will determine their chosen path; and to those who yearn to understand the violence on our city streets, they offer a path to salvation as a model for a better way.

Father David Kelly C.PP.S. – Precious Blood of Ministry of Reconciliation. Doctoral Thesis -- "Responding to Violence among Urban Youth: A Restorative Approach."

Acknowledgement

We thank "Allah" for giving us the gift of life. It's only because of "Him" that we are still standing strong and are the men we are today. All thanks go to the most "High." We also give thanks to everyone who believed in us, stood by us, and even to those who have hurt us, gave up on us, and spoke ill of us. The doubters inspired us to never give up, and even though we are incarcerated, we can make a difference.

Apologies

We apologize for our part in keeping the cycle of violence alive on the streets of Chicago, Illinois. When we were living that lifestyle, we hurt people, damaged our neighborhoods, and fed the violence that continues to destroy our children and community. This book is our way of saying we are sorry, and that we want to make a positive contribution to society.

Table of Contents

Death or a Prison Cell

Introduction..13

Origin..17

Self-Hate...21

Indoctrination..24

Self-glorification..29

Bogus Religion...33

Opposition..36

Warfare..39

Retaliation..44

Violation..48

Criminal Addiction..52

Residue...56

Isolation..60

Rebirth

A Place for Hope..66

Love...69

Empathy...74

Education...78

Humility...82

Spirituality...86

Peace..89

Forgiveness...93

Compassion..97

Legit Hustle..100

Unity...103

Communication...106

Destination..109

Chicago Gangs

Chicago Gangs: Then & Now...114

Chicago Gang, Prison, and a Better Life..125

Epilogue..140

Glossary..151

Death or a Prison Cell

Young Blood

Young blood, you think it's cool to run the streets,

selling drugs, poisoning people, packing the heat.

You fool, that shit ain't cool.

Finish school, train your mind,

rebuild your community for the people behind.

Young blood, you think it's cool,

Ridin' dubs, rocking gear, sportin' some tail.

You a fool, that shit ain't cool.

Open your eyes, lift your head,

else you end up in the pen, or likely dead.

Adolfo Davis

Introduction

"We beat and kill people," the boy confessed. Those words jumped out at us while reading an article on child soldiers in Africa. We had been assigned the story in our House of Healing class at the Stateville maximum-security prison in Joliet, Illinois. Stanley Davis, was making a presentation on the similarities between child soldiers and American teen gang bangers. The facial expressions of the child soldiers mimicked the look of anger and despair in our urban youth. Apparently *mean-mugging* is the universal way of expressing one's frustration whether in the American ghettos or a civil war in the Congo of Central Africa. The young gang bangers and child soldiers were being turned into criminals, drug-addicts and murderers as if they were products of some grand plan to destroy the world.

The three of us – Adolfo Davis, Stanley Davis, and Patrick Pursley – are each serving a life sentence for murder, and have spent over half of our life in a maximum-security prison. The street gangs served as incubators for the development of our criminal behavior. But decades in a prison cell allowed us to ponder the twists and turns our life path has taken. One might say that we have discovered the secrets to a meaningful life. It is time that we share those secrets and make a positive contribution to society.

Our class was working on a form of school therapy designed to prevent inner-city youth from following a path of guns, gangs, crime, violence, drugs and death. Presentations revolved around restorative justice, inner change and life transformation.

Stan's presentation outlined four points that child soldiers and gang members experience: Indoctrination, opposition, warfare, and residue. We expanded the four points to create the 12-step workbook, illustrating how the street culture sucks you in, like wastewater down a city drain. At the conclusion of the 12-step program, we offer a healing path. If not taken, you will join the forgotten; locked in a secluded cell; perhaps murdered at a young age and left rotting in an unmarked grave. We conclude with a discussion on the workings of the Chicago Gangs, then and now.

Today's troubled youth have a belief system void of moral values. A street culture of *gangs, swag, bling, fast drug money, poppin' pills, drinking, smoking weed, trickin' off and street respect* are considered to be more valuable than an education, career, marriage, kids, and a future. Our youth are drawn into a life style of gang banging, selling drugs, and a criminal-minded mentality.

So many *shorties* go from being a *wanna-be* to becoming *deep in the streets*. From catching petty cases to saying things like, "I ain't goin' back to jail unless it's for murder." Then he catches that murder case and gets 60-years or natural life and still can't wake up. When he's 50 years old and into 30-years of prison time, he's still talking gang stuff. A lot of dudes in prison are still hollerin' about what they used to do in the 80's and 90's. But now they have no money, no job, no visits and their family has turned their back on them.

Some still talk about their heyday when the movie *Superfly* came out in the 70's. The star, Youngblood Priest, was a cocaine dealer who realized that his life would soon end in prison or a bullet to his head. He decided to build an escape plan from his troubled-life by selling 30 kilos of cocaine and using the money to start a crime-free life.

The problem is that the mob did not have a retirement plan, leaving a choice of selling drugs for them or becoming stone dead. Nearly every character in the film tries to dissuade Priest from quitting; the chief argument being that dealing and snorting are the best he ever could achieve in life. In the end, Priest was lucky. He managed to walk away with his girlfriend, Georgia.

While a segregated prison cell can be lonely at best, it provides the setting to ponder the twists and turns our path has taken. We now see the errors of our ways, and share the secrets to a better life. This is our gift to you.

Origin

Even the most unrepentant assailants, the most cold-blooded murderers, the most sadistic of serial killers, were once infants. There was a time when they could barely hold a rattle, much less a gun; when they smiled for Christmas portraits and giggled at peek-a-boo; when they were afraid of fireworks, needed help to feed themselves, and wore shoes no bigger than ring boxes. What happened? What inner or outer factor – parents, schools, genes, morals, abuse, television, neglect, stress, attention deficits, self-esteem, and temperament – has the power to transform innocence into violence? The answer provided by modern neuroscience is "all of the above."

The Biology of Violence by Debra Niehoff

***

What you ride? Where you from? That's what they ask when you go to jail. Most conversations go like this, *Yeah, you know dude over there on that block?*

Yeah, I used to be over there and my 'ol girl moved over there when I was a shorty.

You know he's dead? What about Jones, you know him?

Yeah, he's in jail, he caught a body.

The gang members want to know what project building and what block you live in. That determines if you are a Disciple, Vice Lord, Stone, King, Blood, or Crip. What unique background brings juveniles together for a common purpose, a perceived road map for survival? Is it predetermined, accidental, or a reflection of their history?

Science tells us that we are products of our DNA and life's experiences. While we can't do much to affect our DNA, there's a whole bunch we can do about our life experiences. Every action and reaction from birth to your current status determines who you are. The damage can begin with the fertilized egg in the mother's womb. Imagine how drugs, physical and sexual abuse affect the mother, and in turn, the unborn fetus.

The human brain is like putty, ready to be molded into a criminal mind. A body with bullet holes and a knife blade to the stomach; poor schools, uneducated parents, and family members living out their life in a prison cell; a sky laced with air pollution, noise and confusion; a daily diet of day-old bread, beans, contaminated water, and the occasion can of soda pop; disease-infested roaches, high amounts of lead, and poor healthcare contribute to your reality.

Whether you are Black, Hispanic, or White, knowing your history gives meaning to your life. No one was put on this planet for the purpose of stealing, lying, fighting, selling drugs, killing, gossiping, talking bad about people and hating others. No one is born to kill. Add street gangs to the equation and you have a drug-addicted inmate seemingly floating down the concrete hallway of a maximum-security prison. His mind is focused on the next med line, or doing any favor for an additional pill or two. They form a unique group sometimes called *the bug crew*.

In spite of drug addiction, gangs, and life in a dysfunctional family there is hope. Neuroscientists now believe that criminal behavior is not a fixed behavior. The human brain has a degree of plasticity, or flexibility, called neurogenesis, which can occur well into adulthood. Intervention, in the form of medical, psychological, and spiritual help is available. Whether you are an atheist, agnostic, or whatever, many turn to a God or spiritual belief to provide meaning to their life.

Discussion Questions for Origin

1) Do you have to live up to the reputation of the *hood.*

2) What did you inherit from the h*ood*?

3) Was there gang violence in your school?

4) Drugs have been in your community forever. Can you envision a time without drugs?

5) How have drugs affected your family?

6) Do your friends use drugs?

7) How many stories have you heard about the good old days in the street and prison gangs?

8) Do the streets tempt you to join a gang?

9) Do they ever talk about the *O.G.'s* and how some died or went to prison?

10) How old were you when you first heard the stories?

11) Are you proud of your gang origin? If you are, explain.

Self-Hate

If you don't love yourself,

you cannot love others.

If you have no compassion for yourself,

you are unable to develop compassion for others.

Dalai Lama

***

The cycle of misery, ignorance and dysfunction are hand-me-downs from one generation to another. Some families sow the seeds of self-hate. *Momma's got to raise two boys by herself; Daddy's in the joint; did Momma wrong; got high and beat her down. Boy, you just like your Daddy, he ain't shit!*

Maybe your situation is a little different. Momma is smokin' that stuff or she's in the mob. People in the crib are getting high, hollering, cursing, and fighting. Going to the corner store can get you shot. You are just a *shorty* and live around *pissy* hallways, vacant buildings, crack whores, and used needles scattered about. School is a war zone. Your hood is filled with dope friends, the police treat you bad, and when you turn on the television you see white people living in clean neighborhoods. It doesn't take long for a *shorty* in the hood to realize that Blacks and Latinos live in hell.

Perhaps you have a mother on drugs and an absentee-father. But your grandmother loves you. Why don't your parents feel the same? How can anyone love the programmed-manikin you have become; no feelings, a stone-cold boy not caring whether he lives or dies, drifting through life with nary a positive thought. But the neighbor gang offers the love, respect, and protection that you crave; a twisted reality shared by others who walk the inner-city streets.

I was 8 years into a natural life sentence when my 12 year-old-daughter wrote to tell me about her messed up life. "Where's my big brother?" she asked. How could I tell her that he didn't give a damn about her? She ended the letter with, "I hate my life. I wish I was never born." I didn't hear from my daughter for another 2 to 3 years, and learned that she had been raped.

Self-hate is created because a child thinks black is bad and white is good. "That nigga' ain't shit", or that bitch ain't shit." I bought into that kind of thinking. Some rape, beat, shoot, stab and murder each other because that person looks like us. When I listen to rap music, the words tell stories about Black men killing other Black men, selling drugs or *dogging* out their women. Minorities are especially vulnerable to the message: Look and act a certain way, and that money satisfies all your needs. Prisons are full of people who bought into this lie.

Discussion Questions for Self-Hate

1) Did you learn hate from television, a book, peers, parents, and gangs, God?

2) Do you feel self-hate? If so, why.

3) Who do you identify with?

4) Do you get angry with yourself or others? If so, why.

5) Do you feel frustrated with your life, or do you feel good about yourself?

6) Do you love your brothers and sisters?

7) Were you abused at home? Physical, emotional, sexual?

8) Did you join a gang for protection?

9) Did you join a gang to sell or do drugs because you were frustrated and depressed?

10) Did you drop out of school? Why?

11) What do you want to do when you grow up?

Indoctrination

Do not indoctrinate your children. Teach them to think

for themselves, how to evaluate evidence,

and how to disagree with you.

Richard Dawkins

***

Every *hood* and every mob has its distinct flavor, look, slang, and style of dress; how they wear their hair and the way they walk. The gang culture is the same in Mexico, Los Angeles, East St. Louis, Chicago, New York, or wherever. Growing up in a gang-controlled *hood* requires following their socially accepted behavior.

Shorties often have a father, uncle, big brother, or some dominate male figure that they want to emulate. Sometimes that involves getting high or drunk, *bagging* up work, loading guns, stashing drugs or merchandise. Sometimes the dominant figure will show *shorty* the gang signs and have him *throw 'em* up to get a laugh. See and learn, that's what children do.

Take the case of the eight-year old Gangster Disciple Queen who got kicked out of school giving a boy oral sex in the school bathroom. The child's father was a Gangster Disciple and had spent his entire life in and out of prison. The father and his children sold drugs out of their project apartment when dope-friends came to *cop crack*. While I was there, I saw the girl smoke joints that were sitting in the ashtray or finish half-bottles of beer left behind. Her physically abused momma smoked crack until the pain disappeared. I heard the little girl scream during one of her mother's beatings. "I told that bitch, daddy!"

There was a 13-year old GD Queen hanging with gangsters twice her age. They took her on *stangs* and pulled off a home invasion where a 12-year old girl recognized the 13-year old. The older girl told the gang that the twelve-year old knew her, and that they should kill her. After unsuccessfully trying to drown the twelve-year old, they stabbed and shot her until her heart beat no more.

Gang indoctrination begins with older dudes giving kids attention. This is the birth of cool. The indoctrination of the *shorties* teaches them a value system that is transformed into slick sayings:

"Books are for lames."
"I gott'a get mines."
"It's all about that grind."
"Paper-chase."
"M.O.B., money over bitches."
"Thug life."
"Till the world blow up."
"I'm a mack."
"I'm a pimp."
"This ain't a gang, it's an organization."
"We don't love them hoes."
"Don't get caught slipp'in."
"I'd rather be judged by 12 than carried by 6."
"Don't sleep."
"Mickey D's ain't paying shit."
"Work is for squares."
I'm out here try'n to eat."

"If I don't sell it to them, someone else will."

While gangs are blamed for poor choices, I was emotionally, mentally, and spiritually damaged before I hit the *block*. I was taught that crying was for *sissys*, homosexuals were bad, don't be a *tella tale*, and that cheating on your spouse was cool.

Gangs program you to believe that school and hard work are for *lames* and *suckers*. And that stealing, killing, and dealing to get fast money is justified no matter who gets hurt. However, all too often, the street code leads young people to an early grave or with a murder case. While most teens lack knowledge of school subjects, they are hooked by the printed words in gang literature. The grand ideas reel them in like fish in a pond.

One boy who was sentenced at fifteen to live in a cage forever, once told me all he can do now is die for something. When he was a boy, he would have died for his gang, because that was all he had. To him, a gang was the closest understanding of love—it was the only alternative to an empty belly and heart. After spending more than half of his life in prison, he has dedicated his life to being a mentor and advocate for young men to have the chance he never had to be a child, to be safe, to be educated, and to be accountable for the violence in their communities. Although the police regularly harassed him, such as picking him up and dropping him off in rival gang territory and *perp-walking* him, he is sincerely (and controversially) compassionate towards the police. He believes black families must be the catalyst for safer policing in disinvested neighborhoods like the one he grew up in, by focusing on the violence in their own communities. He suggests gang members must understand that being killed because of the color of their skin is not so different from killing someone based on the color their shirt.

Many young gang members drop out of school, and don't have the knowledge to scrutinize the street literature. The average dude off the block thinks that it sounds slick and gives them a purpose and something to believe in. All religions, politics, wars, cult leaders throughout history use ideas and slogans to indoctrinate and control their followers. Gang indoctrination is a system of mind control, providing justification for its existence.

Discussion Questions for Indoctrination

1) Most street youth are in gangs and exposed to a system of indoctrination. Do these principles benefit the member or community?

2) Loyalty is a fundamental part of the indoctrination. Sometimes you are arrested because you are a gang member, not because you actually committed the crime. Are other gang members loyal to you and speak the truth, or would they let you rot in prison?

3) The old saying, "each one teach one," keeps the gangs in place. What do you teach your little brother, sister, neighborhood kids, school friends and school drop-outs?

4) Do you ever feel that your parents can't tell you anything, that the streets are in your blood? Do you ever hate coming home because your parents are telling you to stay away from your friends? Are they wrong? Explain.

5) Do you feel that you are a man at 15-years old and that your parents are not needed any longer? Do you feel that your *homies* will look out for you? Do you want to quit school and hang out on the corner?

Self-Glorification

One of the things that people sense is that you are

not doing this for self-glorification, you are doing

it for the sake of others.

The Dalai Lama has been in exile for so many years,

yet the Chinese are running scared of him.

Desmond Tutu

***

Some label Black men as niggers, criminals or low life's. Over time, we adopted these titles, believed and glorified them to the fullest. Gang life and street values teach young men to *puff* themselves up with pride. It's cool to *swag* and pretend to be the *baddest.* "I can beat your ass, my gun is bigger, my clothes are colder, my diamonds *bling* brighter, my *whip* is super bad, I have sex with five star chicks every night, my money is *longer* than yours and I smoke the *baddest cush.* This is a typical dude out on the streets going nowhere; some *chief* drops off the work and the dude is underpaid; or working a dope spot and living in fear of the police. The little money he makes is spent on weed, liquor and over-priced gear. After a year or two in the game he catches a case and doesn't have the money to hire a lawyer. After sitting up in the County, he finds out his guys told on him. He goes to trial, is found guilty and sent to prison for 60 years.

In the joint he gets to watch rap videos and wish for a life he will never have. One day he gets the news that his chief, the one who put the packs and pistols in his hand, is still out there rolling but hasn't taken the time to send him a money order. Still, after all of this, the gang dude will not let go of that old self-glorification and tells war stories about all of his freak sex and money he never had, and brags about the dudes he shot and beat up. If his chief is still out there, he still throws around his name. "Yeah, I used to get money with him."

This is the lifestyle of the average gang member that doesn't get killed. He sits in prison 20 to 30 years talking about what he used to do, still bragging about the gang mess. To his family and society, he's a loser. But in his own brain, he's a legend. When you mix self-hate with indoctrination, you get self-glorification; an out-of-control ego that finds a way to say, "I'm important, I'm a real bad man."

How do I know all of this? When I was gang-banging in the early 80's, I was the coolest; burglarizing, robbing, pimping, selling drugs, fighting, walking around with a sawed off shotgun, wearing trench coats and *gangsta' brims*. I was breaking safes down in the projects, driving hotrods, Cutlasses, and Monte Carlos'. And now, here I am, age forty-four with natural life. My son doesn't talk to me. My youngest daughter's momma won't let her in my life. Back in the day, I beat my chest and *threw* it up. I was a gangster! But in reality, I was a petty criminal throwing my life away for a bunch of dudes who stole from me, tried to *sex* my girl, and sent detectives to my door because the dudes told on me.

I've looked back on my foolishness and self-glorification, and watched the ego of the average gang member grow even larger. Gang members upload their videos on YouTube and Facebook. They have BET and VH1 that play movies like "New Jake City," "Menace to Society," "Boy'z-n-The Hood," and "Paid in Full" that feed their ego's and glorify their lifestyle. Rap music pumped via radio and videos, gangsta' rap images, diamond grills, fat and killing niggas', it's reality.

The images you see and hear are the devil trying to blind you from who you can become. Stop taking in the propaganda that all black kids are criminals, gangbangers, dead-beat dads, gold-digger women. You are better than that.

Discussion Questions for Self-Glorification

1) Why do you think drug dealing is worth the risk?

2) Do you think selling drugs and possibly getting hurt in the process or hurting someone else in order to buy things is worth prison time?

3) Do you like the power of carrying a gun and power over people?

4) Do you glorify your gang's chief? How much are you willing to do for him? More than you would do for your parents?

5) Are you proud of destroying your 'hood?

6) How do you feel about the killings associated with you and your gang?

7) Are you proud of being a part of an organization that shoots a little boy or girl for no reason?

8) Do you raise your head high when you hear about a schoolgirl getting raped by an addict you sold drugs to?

9) *Bling* that belongs to you can cause a lot of damage because you wanted to glorify your gang. How does that make you feel?

Bogus Religion

You can speak with spiritual eloquence,

Pray in public, and maintain a holy appearance...

But it is your behavior that will reveal your true character.

Dr. Steve Maraboli

***

Religion is a powerful weapon when placed in the hands of misguided individuals, and is sometimes used as a means of controlling people. Not unlike religion, gangs use ideas and symbols to further their agenda.

In today's world the Taliban and Al Qaeda use religion to motivate and control their followers. In the United States, the KKK was a group that claimed to be Christian yet tortured and killed Blacks. While gangs rarely call themselves a religious group, they often use slang, literature, and symbols in their literature such as the six pointed star of David, a cross, a pyramid with an eye over it, a five pointed star and crescent moon. In Chicago, it's all about whether you are under the five or six point star. Symbols tie individuals to something greater than themselves, and can be used in either a positive or negative manner.

If your gang brings death and destruction, the religious ideas, images, and prayers in your literature are for show. I know plenty of killers with *iced* out Jesus pieces, tattoos of the Virgin Mary, and five-point stars with crescent moons. They might call themselves Christians or Muslims, quote the Koran or Scripture, but the love in their soul is hidden by their violence. Individuals are loyal to their mob, not the religious ideas they spout.

When it's time to ride and a gang war breaks out, those members are shooting and

stabbing with a bogus-religious zeal.

Discussion Questions for Bogus Religion

Write a page on how gangs and religion are connected, and what effect it has on its gang members.

Opposition

When the enemy opposes us as he surely will,

We should respond with prayer, work, vigilance,

And focus on the Lord.

Nehemiah 4: 1-23

***

In the gang culture, anyone who does not think like us is the Opposition. "This is our block. Them dudes on the other block are the enemy." You are controlled by what your chief says you should believe. Anything or anyone who threatens your perceived reality is the opposition, and should be eliminated. The fear can be based on the color of their skin, how they dress, the position of their caps, or anything that is different from your culture. You become a prisoner of your block, afraid to venture into the other territory.

I remember when these things were connected with racism. We, as black men, couldn't use restrooms for whites; no relationships with white women; segregated schools, segregated neighborhoods. We killed each other based on the color of our skin. But opposition went to another level when they killed because of the color of their clothes, and because gangs believed they are better than the opposition.

The police use gang opposition to coerce and get information from you. If you don't cooperate, they put you in their car and drive you to the opposition's 'hood and make you get out. The night air crackles when their mega-phone announces, "Yeah, we got a disciple for y'all." You will be running for your life.

When you are taught to hate someone so much that you kill them without a second thought, that is the ultimate form of mind control. Gang chiefs are skilled at working the concept of opposition into the minds of the *shorties*. I knew a young brother who caught his murder at sixteen. He along with a twelve and fourteen-year old boy were standing on a corner. One says, "yeah, them disciples were up there talking about you." The sixteen-year old asked, "You want me to go kill him?"

The sixteen-year old killed a member of the disciples with a gunshot to the head. He was sentenced to seventeen years in prison. Fear and hatred for the opposition cost each his life. One boy dead, the other's life was damaged forever.

Living in brother and sisterhood is the opposite of what opposition stands for and it is the idea behind what life is all about. Brother and sisterhood is understanding that the dudes who are in a different gang still live in the same slums, attend the same school and have the same messed up home life. They face the same judges and jails when they catch their *case*. They wear the same clothes, have the same struggles and have ancestors that might have rode the same slave ship, snuck across a border or came across on a steamer struggling to make a better life for their kids.

Brother and sisterhood makes you understand that everyone is going through the same experience because we're all human beings, came to this world with nothing and leaving with nothing. We're all together in this thing called life. All that matters is realizing the true enemy is not in someone else, but in the people misleading you. This is the true opposition.

Discussion Questions for Opposition

1) When you were branded the "opposition," did you become a target of a street organization?

2) If you refuse to join a gang, what are the consequences? Are you the opposition?

3) Are individuals you go to school with who are not in a gang your opposition?

4) Are your parents – who don't belong to the gang – your enemy?

5) Are the people in your neighborhood who fight against gangs and drugs your enemy?

6) Is the rest of society your opposition? If so, explain.

7) Society believes that youth who belong to a gang are involved in anti-social behavior. Agree or disagree? Explain.

8) Gang fights and violence are often against the "opposition," the truth is that it is against your brother/sister – how can you resolve the hatred toward them?

9) How can we use the word opposition to mean something positive?

10) Do you truly hate your brother/sister to the point of murdering them because somebody told you to do so?

Warfare

The law of the street is to take,

or be taken.

Anonymous

***

Youngsters, and even babies get caught in crossfire when gang members start shooting into a crowd. Society looks at black males with fear and hatred. "There goes the neighborhood," people say when poor minorities move in. All of the pain and abuse we suffer from our childhood comes out in warfare. The anger, rage, powerlessness and hopelessness explode. Those who feel this despair, relish taking lives and passing their torment onto others. Warfare and the mob take the community hostage. People are afraid to leave their home.

In the 50's and 60's, gang warfare started as a means of protecting turf. In the 70's, a movie called "Warrior" took gang warfare to a new level. "Cooley High," filmed in Chicago, was another 70's movie. Those attending the movie might exchange words. Perhaps one guy said, "Oh yeah, you and what army?" Another guy responds, "this army…Disciples!" Gang banging was no longer just about protecting the block. It was conquest and self-glorification.

Fighting can be another way of showing off for the girls. This was the gang banging I was used to. Weapons of choice were bats, knives, chains, bricks, bottles, fists, and feet. There would be 20 to 40 guys meeting and going at it for no other reason than the other group was the opposition. As brutal as this might sound, tearing the club up or turning the party out was nothing compared to the level of violence that is being waged in the streets today. In my day, you might get scuffed up and bloody but at the end of the night you made it home. In a crowd you might have one guy with a .22 caliber handgun with two bullets in the chamber. But he never used it.

In the 80's and 90's, movies like "Boys in the Hood," "Menace II Society," and "New Jack City" were released. This was when the game changed. Crack cocaine and guns flooded the *'hood*. While it used to be all about drugs being sold by older dudes, warfare was killing. Major companies began pushing *gang'sts* rap and music that provided a backdrop to *drive-bys*. Warfare was about kids selling *crack, weed, and blows*, and protecting their turf from other gangs.

A culture of death swooped down upon American ghettos. S*horties* became messengers of death. Lyrics of murder were on their lips. The manifestation of evil took young kids like Chicago's Yummy Sanderford and made him a killer at the age of eleven. Yummy was dead before he turned 12. Warfare is the beast that unleashes the worst in us.

When the federal government declared war on drugs, they were declaring war on thugs. In the 80's, President Reagan encouraged news media to show inner-city drug crimes in order to get Congress to put up the loot to fund the "War on Drugs" campaign. The president's actions increased the drug war, encouraged kids to listen to rap music and watch movies that glorified the lifestyles of gangbangers. At the beginning of the "War on Drugs," there were 600,000 people in prison nationwide. Twenty years later, our prison population is approximately 2.3 million people.

Wars are fought by our youth. Older politicians call for war and send the young off to fight and die. This is true for gangs on the street. Chief's put *packs* and guns into the hands of children and send them off to kill the opposition. Their lack of shooting skills leaves an innocent child or bystander dead. *Shorties* are fighting for nothing more than to put money in the chief's pocket or support their drug habit.

When a major gang war broke out between the Gangster Disciples and the Black Disciples, young people were expected to throw their lives away and go to war over anything from drug *spots* to a girl being disrespected. Today, gangs no longer protect their communities, their women or children. War-mongering tendencies destroy both themselves and the innocent.

Many who survived gang wars tell their stories with pride. Men talk about who they beat, stabbed or shot. In jail cells all around me I hear them relive their memories and speak fondly as they tell their stories over and over not realizing that it was through gang warfare that they caught their case and life sentence. They proudly share their tales in the chow hall or the yard. In their heads, they are legends, action heroes with guns blazing. Their ego finds meaning and power in taking lives.

Behind the wall they are just another name and number, but in their minds, they are a playground legend. Ninety-nine percent of the time, their own guys testified against them and here they sit in prison begging for a *noddle*, broke, starving and still gangbanging. They don't realize that society and their own families do not consider them a hero but regard them as fools. Their folly is soon forgotten, except by the families of the men and women they left behind or the families of those they murdered.

I was 15-years old when I joined a gang. I wasn't into it with anyone. Then in a blink of an eye, I was at war with another gang, and 27 years later that war continues and I don't know why. People have been killed or incarcerated, and communities and families have been destroyed over nothing. When you go to prison, you sometimes become best friends with the members of the gang you were out there fighting. That's a reality check.

Discussion Questions for Warfare

1) When you hear that a war has broken out between rival gangs, do you fear sitting on your front porch? Do you fear a drive-by shooting?

2) Do you fear wearing a certain color in certain neighborhoods? Do you fear going to school or to the store?

3) As a gang member, how do you prepare for war?

4) How do you protect yourself from being a victim of gang warfare?

5) Gang warfare includes recruiting someone to be a gunner, someone who might kill innocent people during shootouts with rival gangs. In light of this, how might you avoid being recruited into a gang?

6) Psychological warfare is a neighborhood mentality captured by a few youth who commit violent acts. The media can contribute to the scare tactics that can overwhelm a parent who believes they are living in a war zone. What can a young adult who is not in a gang do to overcome the negative news that comes out of their neighborhood and reclaim it for the positive?

7) Do you feel society is waging a war against you because of your race?

Retaliation

"Vengeance is mine, sayeth the Lord."

Romans 12:19

"He who sets out to get revenge should begin by digging two graves."

Confucius

***

Gang members love the thrill of the kill. They are about catching some fool creeping through a yard and coming out *dumping*. *Hard heads* roll up in a *trap* car and let the opposition have it. Dudes are running, hollering, dropping, and dying. They don't care about the blue box police cameras attached to light poles. Everyone flees, tires squeal, hitting corners, and leaving a trail of destruction. Guns are stashed in the *crib*. Getting drunk and high are the norm.

"Man, did you see that nigga'? I hit 'em in the face. He ain't know what hit him." Some gang bangers really love this life, and know death on a first name basis. The next couple of days the heat is on, and the hit is all over the news. Two gang bangers dead and a seven-year old girl is in a coma with a bullet lodged in her head. The news report says that even if she survives, she will have severe brain damage. This doesn't concern you? But y'all a little nervous until the police say they have no suspects. It's a little hot, but your boys keep their mouths shut for now.

A few days pass. After a session of *blunts, broads, and peptone* you share some laughs and stumble out of the crib at 2 a.m. Things are quiet and you ain't worried. The last thing you are thinking about is that *stang* from the other night. You get in your car and that's when you notice some movement out of the corner of your eye and wonder what's up. You hear a voice. "That was my brother you killed," he yells. You are too drunk to understand what he said. You turn around to see one of the opposition holding a *desert eagle* up to your face. You are numb. The last think your eye registers is the flash of a hand *cannon*. The bullet tears the back of your scalp off as a three inch hole opens up, sending your final thoughts and a greyish pink mist of blood and brains across the windshield of your Chevy.

You never have a chance to tell your baby or mom goodbye. Think about it. You are dead at 19. Your life is over. While you brought it on yourself, it's a lesson that you will never appreciate. It is a universal law: What you put out comes back to you. Your boys will get them and kill a couple more dudes, and by the end of the summer, a couple of your *homies* will join them.

The cycle plays out every day in gangland America; fuels itself and quickly gets out of control. I knew a *homie* who was into retaliation, but his crew was weak. The other gang wasn't playing games, and they killed one of his guys. After that, the opposition caught him at a crap game. He called his *rides* to bring the guns, but their scary selves didn't come. My *homie* survived that night and his boys got together the next day and were going to take care of the opposition, but the police caught him with a pistol and sent him to jail while his enemies struck his crib. They kicked in the door and killed a friend and wounded his baby girl. Since they were not found for several days, his little girl died of dehydration. My *homie* realized that he wasn't just arrested; he was rescued. Had he not gone to jail he would have been killed. Fortunately for him, the cycle was broken. He got out of jail, left that life behind, got a job, a girl, and a crib.

When locked in a violent cycle, you are pushed to be a loyal soldier. You are mad that your man got *merked*. You can't show your fear or think that you are bulletproof. If you can't get out of it, you might be killed or end up in prison fighting a double murder.

I know two *sets* who were at each other hard out east. One side hit the other, the other struck back. Each side kept taking losses and catching cases, going to jail. The cycle got so out of hand that as one mob was having a party to raise money for the family to pay for their murdered *brothas'* funeral, the opposition came and shot up the party. The gang members at the party panicked and returned fire, killing some of their own people. By the time the war was over, both sides were either dead or in prison. Years later, after they told on each other, they sit in prison with natural life, swapping affidavits so they can escape the drama they created. The cycle of opposition, warfare, and retaliation leads you to a dead end.

Discussion Questions for Retaliation

1) Is it wrong to be vindictive because somebody hurt you?

2) How does it feel when you get revenge? Good, bad, thrilling, emotional?

3) When you see a mother on television saying she wants retribution for her son or daughter's murder, can you understand that? How would you feel?

4) What would you do if you committed a crime and a neighbor told on you and you were sent to prison? What would you do when you saw them again?

5) Many children growing up in a poverty-stricken neighborhood might suffer verbal and physical abuse in their home. They become angry and hateful toward others. Violence can be a tool to satisfy their anger. While it makes them feel good, other people are hurt in the process. How do you begin to address the real problem?

6 Do you feel like a victim because of the abuse you experienced? Has your neighborhood, parents, or society made you a victim?

7) List 10 words associated with how you feel about your life when you read this?

8) Do you feel that you are right and do not need to change?

9) If you have children, do you want this life style for them?

10) If you are in a gang at the present time, will they let you change?

11) Part of a street organization is to retaliate against rival gangs. Will you participate?

12) Change means to get rid of the anger inside you and seek help. Are you willing to open up about your life and change?

Violation

Violations could be handed out weekly for breaking Gangster Disciples' Laws. When a riot broke out in one yard in late 1985, two GD members violated GD law to "aid and assist," and both had to be hospitalized from the beating they endured.
As reported by Matt O'Connor, staff writer, Chicago Tribune

***

No matter how religious or political a gang claims to be, they are about brutality, violence, and fear. When it comes to controlling their own, there is no better tool than violation, a means of punishing fellow gang members for breaking the rules. Gangs have an organizational block-by-block structure within the city, and this is true in prison as well. There is a pecking order that maintains power of the members.

When I was coming up in the gang, I thought they loved me. Besides the companionship, money, drugs, protection, and power, there were the beatings they gave me for my own good. When asked why the beatings were so severe, they said it was because I had broken the rules. As in society, those in charge often times violate the rules. But as a follower you obey without exception. The same holds true for prison and street gangs.

Violations can be minor like a fine or harsh workout. But more often than not, a violation is about beating you down. A beating can be a simple punch to your face, something I experienced when I refused to carry out an order to have all my gallery brothers in prison boil water to scald one person. Sometimes I was ordered to stand in a circle while four gang members beat on me.

In prison, violations are extremely violent. Pipes bust you up and crack your skull; knives or shanks cut into your flesh; broken bones are commonplace; and broken teeth fall to the concrete floor. Maybe they give you a "pumpkin head deluxe:" black eyes, broken nose, and a bloody mouth. But when it's over, they pick you up and share the love. But this is not love. This is self-hate.

I sometimes wonder if this goes back to growing up in an abusive family when we didn't know anything else. The more twisted the chief's childhood, the more brutal the beatings became. Some chiefs make up charges because they don't like you. Or perhaps the *shorty* doesn't fit in and is continually subjected to violation.

Some members get favoritism. No matter what they do, they never get violated. In prison there is the chief who is secretly gay but acts super tough and has people beaten on a regular basis. He will spot a young fresh-faced kid and befriend him. This chief will then step in when it's time for the *shorty* to get beat up and tell him, "You know you owe me *shorty*." Later on, the chief will cuff the kid and get him high. *Shorty* will look up to *big homey* as a father, and when the time is right, the chief will say, "Man, you know it's time for you to return the favor." The next thing you know, the chief is getting *shorty* to give him *head* or *going up in shorty*.

Some of the most common violations on the streets deal with money. Gangs make the members pay dues or the chief requires them to sell *mob packs* (drugs) or spend one day a week selling drugs. Sometimes members will *jack* the money off with *hypes* or getting high themselves. The gang isn't hearing any of this. If you mess up the cash, you will be beaten with a baseball bat then put in the trunk of a burning car.

In just about every gang, there are people who rebel and refuse to accept a violation. They are called renegades. Renegades have caused major wars. Most of the time, the gang hierarchy will call a violation to the renegades. This violation isn't about bone crushers beating your brains out. It's the ultimate violation – death. Usually it's some extreme form of torture leading to your death. I knew a renegade who was running around sticking up and extorting his old gang. He had a little crew with him and would get into shoot-outs with his own nation. Evidently this guy thought he was untouchable until his cousin got him drunk and high. The renegade was later found dead with his penis and testicles cut off and shoved in his mouth. His hands and feet were cut off as well. This type of torture killing sends a message to all would-be renegades who disobey the gang leaders.

Discussion Questions for Violation

Breakings rules or laws have consequences. When children break house rules they are disciplined. When we break society's rules, we might face jail. But when gang rules are broken, it could lead to death.

1) Say your baby brother joins the gang, and the two of you get caught because your baby brother told the police. Now the gang wants to violate him. Do you try to stop them?

2) Just because your parents discipline you doesn't mean they hate you. When the gang violates you, it doesn't mean they love you. Whose disciple is for your good? Your parents or the gang.

3) What is the difference between your parent's home rules and the rules of the gang?

4) Did you ever violate a gang member? How did it feel?

5) Do you have any inner principles or values that you would not cross even if the gang asked you to?

6) Do you take part in exploiting your neighborhood because of the gang? Are you violating the people who live there?

7) If you live in an impoverished neighborhood, do you believe that society has violated you?

Criminal Addiction

People commit crimes because of the adrenaline rush,

And they, in turn, become addicted to the adrenaline.

And when that happens, that is when most crimes occur.

Anonymous

***

Why is it fun to do bad things? Why is it boring to do good things? The Holy Quran states that Satan makes evil seem alluring. Criminal addiction involves fighting, mob action, assaults, property damage, curfew violations, public intoxication, possession of drugs, unlawful use of weapons, stolen vehicles, burglaries, robberies, home invasion, possession with intent to deliver a controlled substance, kidnapping, sexual assault, murder. To the gang, doing bad things is cool. It's their reality.

While I didn't want to be a criminal, survival sometimes creates your path. I stole food because we barely had enough to eat. Next were the clothes people hung out to dry on their back porch. But then one day when I went to school sporting my new clothes, someone called me out saying, "Hey Dude, those are my clothes." After he told me that his name was inside the shirt, I got so mad that I beat him up. I moved on to steal anything and everything from stores. Food, toys, clothes, shoes; anything I could carry. I moved on to bikes, cars, jewelry, and even the occasional dog. All of this prepared me for the day I joined a gang. Although selling drugs for the gang was easy money, I continued my addiction to stealing other things.

The streets teach kids to "do whatever you have to, to get yours." *Shorties* see their big brothers, uncles, fathers, or older dudes on the block with their guns and hear gunshots. Gang activity comes from their *cribs* or outside their project windows; an environment where boys become men. Poor kids get new gear, the drug dealer gets a new *whip* and a five-star chick. *Hood* life intrigues a child and becomes a lawless game that draws him in. The first time he holds a gun, a sense of power rushes through him. Television, movies, video games and the streets teach him what gang leaders want – power.

These are steps to criminal addiction. "Gimme some money or I'll shoot you!" A five year old taunts his mama's new boyfriend as he points a toy gun at him. He learns about sex and curse words on rap that blasts throughout his *crib*. By ten, he's fighting, stealing, and trying to *freak* little girls on the block. By now, he's a *Shorty* getting high, drunk, and having a blast. When he reaches 12 or 13, he's hustling, shooting, and all the things that gang members do.

An inner voice kicks in when we get ready to do something bad. Perhaps it's our conscious or the voice of God. But a *shorty* moves past those feelings. When he sets out to steal something, his heart races and his pulse quickens. While he knows that it is wrong, he wants it so bad. The kid gets away with it and feels the rush that the criminal mind craves. "I'm slick, I'm smart." Stealing has cost him his innocence. He has broken the law for the first time.

The next thing you know, *shorty* is stealing stuff and the voice of God is gone. In time, the *shorty* has grown in stature, and moves into more violent acts. But his heart has hardened and the thrill has diminished. He feels the need to experience violence without limits. Only then does he feel the rush again. It's like a crack-head chasing that first high. It doesn't matter if you're robbing or dealing, the power of the gun is addictive, much like the power that a drug dealer feels when everyone is *jocking* and kissing his butt, when he can get any woman he wants with his bank roll, *bling and ride.*

Everything I've described is a process, a slippery slope that leads to an illusion of a wicked paradise. Each step down the criminal path leads to hell. Criminal addiction is 100 times worse than a drug or alcohol problem because crime hurts other people. It's like throwing a rock across the surface of a pond. Ripples become waves, and evolve into a tsunami of devastation. The universal law says, "What you put out comes back at you." In science, it's called "cause and effect." No one is born evil; it's a step-by-step process; a seduction that leads to addiction. It's a life that seldom makes you think, "Okay, this is the last *brick*, the last *stang* and I'm out." It ends like this – most of us get out by going to jail or being killed. Criminal addiction corrupts and stains the soul; puts a veil over our eyes; and hides the light and glory of the Creator.

Discussion Questions for Criminal Addiction

1) Innocent children are murdered by stray bullets and violent acts. What can we/you do to stop this?

2) Criminal addiction is a disease that manifests itself through a person's anger, poverty, low self-esteem and joining a gang. How can a person overcome all of these things without committing crimes?

3) Do you believe you were born to be a criminal because someone in your family has been in jail?

4) Do you believe that if you are poor, live in a project, a reservation, or a trailer park you have no choice but to become addicted to crime.

5) Do you think you or anyone can overcome the crime that's in your heart?

6) What makes us commit crimes?

7) Is society or you responsible for crime?

8) Most criminals commit multiple crimes and have been to prison more than once. Are they addicted to crime?

9) Do you feel that criminal activity is the result of instability in the lives of individuals involved in crime or has society given them a raw deal?

Residue

The system locked up and killed off all of the Kings and "Super Chiefs." Their gangs were broken into pieces and chaos on the streets. There is nothing left on the streets but residue.

While talking about residue in street terms, most people think about some crack-head cleaning out his pipe with alcohol and trying to scrape that last little hit from the plate. Gang residue is more potent than any hit from a crack-head's pipe. It is the last of the last.

For *shorties* growing up in the era of residue, it's hard to imagine anything other than 15 year olds running around spraying the block with AKs. In the past several years, Chicago street gangs have killed more school students than any other city in the United States. The killers are teenagers, and are more potent than their daddy's were in their day. In the early days, gangs gave birth to some chiefs or kings who had larger than life personalities. On the west coast was Stanley "Tookie" Williams of the Crips, the east coast had Africa Bambata of the Zulu Nation and Chicago had Willie Lloyd, Larry "King" Hoover and Jeff Fort. These men helped create some of the most notorious gangs in the states. They demanded loyalty, discipline, following the code of the streets and keeping their gang members in line. Criminals were older, and kids were not killing. Gangs said that you were a punk if you couldn't throw your hands. The weapons of choice were bricks, bottles, knives, and whatever. Dudes went at it hard. But at the end of the fight you made it home alive.

Gang structure was solid. There was basic and genuine concern for their members. But things changed by the late '80s. While large gangs were dismantled and smaller, more violent gangs took over. Allegiances and lines were crossed. People flipped folks, and folks flipped people. Crack, high-powered weapons and stiff prison sentences destroyed the large gang structure. Drug profits went through the roof, leading to a sudden flow of automatic weapons to kill off the competition. Those left on the streets were loose cannons that would kill over loose change, and many times for nothing.

***

I was raised in an unstable home -- no father, and a mother who loved drugs more than their kids. The Department of Children and Family Services (DCFS) knew that my home was not fit for me to live in. But they kept me there like left over residue. So, I turned to the streets where I met other kids who were looking for a place to fit in. We became a family where we learned to survive, which led to joining a gang. This was the family that we had searched for. Then the police locked up all of the gang chiefs or killed them. That left the members with no guidance. Again, we were residue, the leftovers.

Then the city knocked down our projects, closed schools, and forced us into other communities. We had to find another place to fit in. But the other communities were not open to the new kids moving in. That's when the fighting moved to another level. We had to fight or die to prove that we belonged. Today, prisons are filled with the children who did not fit in.

I can't help but believe that this was some type of plan to push us into a corner and let us kill each other. Please don't become victims like so many of us. The system is not designed for us. We know this but we still fall victim. As a result, we have left our children behind because of decisions and actions that we took.

Discussion Questions for Residue

1) What residue are you left with from your relationship with the gang?

2) Do you believe that street terrorists are productive to society?

3) What do you think your community thinks of you when you become a gang member?

4 How do your parents feel if you commit a crime? Have your parents committed crimes with you?

5) Have your parents used drugs with you? If they did, how did you feel about that?

Isolation

Solitude, isolation, are painful things,

And beyond human endurance.

Anonymous

***

Origins, self-hate, indoctrination, self-glorification, bogus religion, opposition, warfare, retaliation, violation, criminal addiction, and residue, – are factors that make a gang member. However, this is not the end of the line. All of this leads to isolation. Accepting street values and becoming a gang member, a petty street thug, and drug dealer will lead to death or prison – cut off and isolated. You lose your freedom, family, and future. When all of the negativity comes back to you and manifests into your life, you suddenly realize that you have created the hell your life has become. If you somehow have managed to survive, there is hope if you see the error of your ways and seek a different path. As long as you are alive, there is hope. There is an old saying, "change your mind, change your world."

Discussion for Isolation

1) Do you have a fear of isolation?

2) Does the choice between death and prison make gangs appear less attractive?

Lost my Soul

Lost in the maze, as I chase my soul.

Did it escape, perhaps run away.

Yearning to touch, feel, or smell

the tangy taste of sweetness.

Did it ever exist.

Lost in the quiet of darkness,

many days gone by,

when Grandma shared lessons of hope and love,

and perhaps the eternal life.

Blown away by the windy city breeze,

When I was the baddest, mean-mugging shortie you ever did see.

Smoking and peddling Chicago's high-quality dope,

Lost my way in that eternal maze.

Adolfo Davis

Change

Times a changing, brothers the same,

Losing their lives to the crazy game.

And now you wonder why I've changed.

Mother shedding tears,

'cause she lost her seed.

Homies prepare to kill,

As they smoke some weed.

And now you wonder why I've changed.

Seasons a mystery outside the prison walls,

Yearning to see colored leaves,

as summer moves into fall.

Time to move, time to forget,

best to die, with no regrets.

And now you wonder why I've changed.

Adolfo Davis

Rebirth

A Place for Hope

Chaos and destruction sent us on a one-dimensional path into darkness. We were unloved, unwanted, abandon, and scared. But the most dangerous emotion was self-pity, the incubator of evil. Feeling sorry for oneself feeds the anger within us. The world owes us, that is how we felt. Two of us blamed our parents for everything bad that happened in our lives. They are the reason we are rotting in prison. Stanley had a different experience. As a young boy, Stanley witnessed a policeman murder his uncle; a scene that continues to be replayed in his memory.

There are the quiet times in prison when broken men sleep at night. Mixed amongst the moments of stillness, there are the curious thoughts: Maybe the gangs were a bad thing; perhaps there's a better way; or if only I had taken responsibility for my choices. These conscious and unconscious thoughts suggest that I could have been a better person; a family man with a wife, children, and a steady job. These are the things that I want, the dreams that suggest a better way.

During 27 years in prison, there are times when the seeds of curiosity attach to your soul. Without proper attention, they fester and destroy you as sure as a dead man walking. This is the time when you think and pray that you find another way. Sometimes the path becomes quick and clear, but the answers are not available in your current mindset. Goodness was shut out by the darkness of evil.

Sometimes we feel like a blind man feeling his way through a maze of alternative paths. Perhaps we need help learning a new way of life. Adolfo and Patrick found their path through Islam while Stanley chose Christianity. Adolfo also discovered his answers from a counselor at the Stateville maximum-security prison. She told Adolfo that he needed to forgive his parents and stop blaming them for all of the bad choices he made. While her suggestions did not immediately take hold, the quiet of a dark cell brought clarity to her advice. This became the time when Patrick, and Stanley decided to make choices that could change their lives forever.

But the answers from Islam, Christianity, and the voice from our counselors are not as simple as a math equation of $2 + 2 = 4$. Determination and a questioning attitude are needed to find a level of understanding. Science tells us that we are the product of our genes and environment. Our history of good and bad choices made us who we are. Change requires us to learn the things we should have been taught during childhood and throughout our life.

Quiet time is needed for the healing process. Anyone traumatized from their history of violence and abuse, needs a place where spiritual needs can be addressed. An outsider might logically consider a chapel, church, mosque, or some holy place as the center for spiritual growth. But the most sacred place is the soul within; the place where God resides; the center of spirituality.

A large part of Adolfo's emotional healing took place when he was transferred to the Tamms supermax prison. Many inmates isolated in a single cell have become great. It was through years of incarceration that brought them to the place where they reached out for help. They made the choice to find a better way. Prison became a place for hope.

Discussion questions for A Place for Hope

1) People seeking spiritual growth and reflection need a place for healing. Where is your place for hope?

2) Do you have a procedure or plan that you follow when reaching into your soul?

Love

Knowing yourself is the beginning of all wisdom.
Aristotle

Know thyself.
Socrates

Love is an emotion that we search for throughout our lives. Prison and street gangs gave us a false sense of love, and created a reality of heartache and self-destruction. We have to ask ourselves what love really means. Love don't kill, love don't destroy, love don't hurt people. Love heals, protects, and is one of the keys to true humanity.

Love is when we put other people's feelings first and begin to feel their pain. Think about how you affect the people you care about. Will your gestures of happiness help or will they create more misery for the other person? When you make someone's life better, you will unknowingly reap positive benefits as well.

Adolfo once said, *I was never taught genuine love. We don't teach love. We don't know how to love no more. I was taught loyalty, but that loyalty became a weapon. People want to be loyal, but that is not love. Love is someone who would do anything to make sure that person does not feel pain. Love is showing a kindness of spirit and being a protector. At the end of the day, I believe we are our worst enemy. Sometimes we need to get away from our family to be the person we know we want to be.*

Love is all-encompassing, requiring self-knowledge to distinguish the difference between self-hate and love of self. A healthy love of self is a love of life. You value your life too much to throw it away doing dumb stuff. You learn to understand your strengths and weaknesses; you learn the history of your people, the values of your culture. Knowing who you are is the first step in understanding your Creator and the connection to your life. When you gain self-knowledge you are changed; you are plugged into your humanity; and when you are approached by negativity, you walk away.

There are many paths that lead to love and happiness. Larry L. Franklin shared his secrets obtained throughout his many years of trial and error. His lessons were unveiled through writings to his grandchildren. Use your imagination and visualize Franklin's path. This was his journey. Perhaps it would work for you.

Seemingly elusive, my path to happiness is really quite simple. First, build yourself a flower garden, preferably one big enough to walk through. Surround it with bird houses, bird feeders, and a bird bath or two.

Pick a shaded area and dig a hole. Place an Ostrich Fern in the hole and fill with a mixture of top soil and dirt. Rub the soil mixture between your fingers, breathe deeply, and let the earth speak to you. Stroke the leaves. Notice the tilted stems, the beauty of a plant without flowers. Move to a nearby spot and plant a Coral Bell with its purple leaves and long stems that hold miniature white flowers. Notice how the Ostrich Fern and Coral Bell complement each other. Add oriental grasses, sedums, a bronze fennel, various shaped rocks, and your personal favorites.

Sit among your newly acquired friends and feel the love, and the presence of God. On any special day, you might be buzzed by a hummingbird, blessed by a bee, have a butterfly land on your head, or listen to a wren sing a lullaby. This is truly important. In a short time, you will have created your flower garden that will attract birds, butterflies, bees, worms, grasshoppers, and more living creatures than you can imagine.

Next buy a dog. Any animal will do but a dog is my favorite. Yours can be of the mixed variety obtained from a humane shelter or a pure blood with official looking papers. It makes no difference: a dog is a dog. I've had five dogs in my life and they all offered the same magnificent gift: unconditional love. Take on the responsibility for the care of your dog, and whether you're arriving or leaving, give your dog a hug. In return, you will receive devotion and love like you never imagined. This, too, is important.

Develop friendships with two, three, or more people who, like your flower garden, come in different sizes, shapes and colors. Be with your friends, as if you were in a temple, where every word and thought are deemed sacred. Freely share gentle hugs while you experience your friends' happiness and sit with their pain. Learn to share your love with the glance of an eye or the touch of a hand.

At times, the temptation to veer from this path will be strong, and some friends may pull away. The currents of instant gratification are powerful. Although they're nice – the expensive house, flashy cars, designer clothes and other such yearnings – they don't match the love found in your flower garden, dog, or best friend. Shun the ways of the noisy parrots who seemingly know what's best. Listen to your heart and continually question yourself. When you've found all the answers, you've lost your way.

A Mother's Love

I searched high and low

but could never find,

the love you held deep inside.

When I looked into your eyes,

I felt nothing but hate.

I wish I had died

And never saw your face.

It's an everlasting nightmare,

I can't escape.

The pain's deeper,

my heart's weaker.

I hate you so much.

Time to move on,

the feelings erased.

But a mother's love,

can never be replaced.

Adolfo Davis

Discussion questions for Love

1) What is love, and what does it mean to you?

2) Have you ever been loved?

3) How do you know who you are?

4) Could you teach your friends how to be more aware of their worth?

Empathy

Empathetic people are less likely to engage in delinquency or crime. But those who have trouble perceiving how others feel, and have difficulty sharing those feelings, are more likely to engage in wrongful acts – everything from minor juvenile delinquency to the most serious of violent crimes.

"The Role of Empathy in Crime, Policing, & Justice
Chad Posick, Georgia Southern University

***

Survival is how we lived on the streets and in the prisons. The last thing you wanted was to look weak. And helping others, or placing their needs above yours, made you look weak. Being strong kept your enemies at arms length. You needed to strut when you walked and sport an angry face. Hurting other people and committing crimes were part of our DNA. Your enemies constantly looked for signs of weakness, and would attack when they saw the opening. That's the way it is in prison and on the streets of Chicago.

When we gangbang, sell drugs, shoot and kill others, we are not considering how our acts of violence affect the victims, their loved ones, and the community. We did not know the meaning of empathy. As far as we knew, empathy could have been the name of a foreign city. To understand and share the feelings of others was not part of our world. But memorizing the definition of empathy does not solve our problem. We must experience the feelings one receives when demonstrating empathy. You will never enjoy the sweetness of a ripen fruit without the act of tasting.

A good place to start is to set aside your opinions, consider the other person's views, and determine whether it is something that you can support. If it requires a bad or illegal response from you, it becomes something you cannot support. Listen, and ask the other person what they would do. While empathy helps us to develop trust, it can lead to serious consequences if not handled correctly.

Science tells us that we are wired to experience empathy through the neurons and neurotransmitters in our brains. This allows us to copy, mimic, or mirror another person's emotions. When we observe someone in pain or in a state of happiness, we experience that to a certain extent. It's a connection to the feelings of the other person. While some people are naturally empathetic, others are not. But research tells us that empathy can be learned.

Most of us who have lived through street and prison gangs tend to have some roadblocks that get in the way. The biggest obstacle is the not knowing how to listen. It's easy to talk and brag and bluster, but listening is a necessary skill. During a conversation, do we know how to listen to the other person? It might seem difficult at first, but you can will yourself in becoming a good listener. Use little tricks like watching their lips move when they are telling, blank out all of the noise around you, turn off the TV or radio while he is talking. Practice listening and it will become natural in time. Remember how frustrating it was while talking to another person and they weren't listening to you. Show interest in what the other person is saying. Offer support by such statements as, "I'm sorry about that, man. I didn't know that you were dealing with that. Tell me what I can do."

Circumstances sometime dictate how we treat others. But we have to move past just thinking about ourselves, and understand that we are not the only ones who have problems. Empathy can change you life. It can change the world.

Questions for Empathy

1) Have you ever heard of the word empathy?

2) Have you ever had empathy for someone in the opposition?

3) Have you ever had empathy for anyone?

Education

We must build a movement for education, not incarceration. A movement for jobs, not jails. A movement that will end all forms of discrimination against people released from prison - discrimination that denies them basic human rights to work, shelter and food.

Michelle Alexander

For people who have committed crimes that have landed them in jail, there needs to be a path back from prison. The federal system of parole needs to be reinstated. We need real education and real skills training for the incarcerated.

Senator Bernie Sanders

***

A study that examined one's longevity, found that people who lived the longest were those who received the most education. The Bible says, "My people are destroyed for lack of knowledge."

The streets tell you what to think, true education teaches you HOW to think. Question your actions and you are more likely not to be fooled by false leaders and political propaganda laid out in gang literature. If we are taught how to think, the trappings of a fast life or easy cash will not fool us.

Education can save your life. It helps you make smarter decisions, avoid negativity, ignorance and people who do stupid stuff. Education not only gets you out of bad situations, it gives you skills that change your life, your future, and the lives of your children.

Rather than continuing the recidivism cycle where inmates serve their time, join the outside world only to return to prison, they should embrace education. Perhaps the fact that inmates are the most poorly educated people in society should not be ignored. Those who participate in education courses while in prison are more likely to stay out of prison when they are released.

According to the editorial board's commentary, *Let Prisoners Learn While They Serve,* published in <u>The New York Times</u>, August 12, 2017, every dollar spent on prison education translates into savings of $4 to $5 on incarceration costs down the line. And prisoners in education programs commit fewer violent acts, making it easier to maintain order and disrupt the typical pattern of poverty and incarceration. As the Manhattan district attorney, Cyrus Vance Jr. said, "It makes no sense to send someone to prison with no pathway for them to succeed." Lessons learned, applies to gang members in and out of prison. There are no limitations on who can improve through education. Without education, it is more difficult to master the steps needed for your path of love and happiness.

Oftentimes people consider education in prison only in terms of reducing recidivism. According to *The Lifelong Learning of Lifelong Inmates,* a June 27, 2017 story written by Clint Smith in <u>The Atlantic</u>, education for lifers creates a more intellectual prison community. Imagine inmates with life sentences studying and sharing thoughts with fellow inmates. There is a degree of intellectual stimulation that broadens the value of each human being, and that applies to lifelong inmates as well. Education can lead to other behavioral attributes such as love, compassion and humility.

Clint Smith shares an excerpt from an essay written by Darryl, a lifelong inmate serving his 43rd year in prison. A small group of inmates sit in a room as they share thoughts with other classmates. One such inmate, Darryl, describes the despair of having the small moments of human relationships stripped away.

I am suffering in this place. Day after day, week after week, year after year, decade after decade, walking up and down hallways; going from room to room in the same building, under surveillance 24 hours a day.

The keepers start the kepts' day off with the intercom announcement at five minutes to 7 a.m. "Five minutes to count! Five minutes to count!" The kept stir to life from a night of visiting who knows what or where, perhaps a dream of being home with mother and siblings or wife and children, sitting at the table to eat a meal of turkey, mashed potatoes with gravy, squash, and cranberry sauce. Then looking down to the end of the table and seeing Taser in hand; turning around and seeing bars on the doorway that was not the same doorway he had entered through.

*Inmate -- **Darryl***

Silence filled the room and an inmate began to nod his head. He looked towards Darryl. "Yea," he said, pausing and then nodding for a few moments. "Thank you."

Education is a human right; a recognition of dignity that each person should be afforded.

Discussion Questions for Education

1) Street education can lead to prison time. How do you educate yourself and not become involved with the criminal element?

2) Gang infested communities have high crime rates. Students are threatened by the violence in school. How can you get past the gangs to obtain a proper education?

3) Parents must get involved in their child's education, and have a better understanding of their needs. How can you educate the community about gangs?

4) Education provides a better life for you and your family. What should you do?

    a) Be a gang member

    b) Be a student

    c) Be a criminal

    d) All of the above

Humility

In reality, there is, perhaps, no one of our natural passions so hard to subdue as pride. Disguise it, struggle with it, beat it down, stifle it, mortify it as much as one pleases, it is still alive, and will every now and then peep out and show itself.

Benjamin Franklin

Pride is concerned with who is right. Humility is concerned with what is right.

Ezra Taft Benson

I have been driven many times upon my knees by the overwhelming conviction that I had nowhere else to go. My own wisdom and that of all about me seemed insufficient for that day.

Abraham Lincoln

Someone I loved once gave me a box of darkness. It took me years to understand that this too, was a gift.

Mary Oliver

***

The opposite of self-glorification is humility. Self-glorification is all about the ego and acting ignorant. Humility puts the ego in check. The Quran says the loudest of voices is like the braying of an ass. Being humble is the opposite of poking out your chest and thinking you are a legend because you sold crack and killed someone. Humility is lowering your spirit before the Creator. It gives you the strength to walk away and more importantly, to not care what others think about you for doing the right thing. When we humble ourselves, all types of doors will open. No one of sound character likes loud, obnoxious, ignorant and arrogant people. To humble oneself is not a sign of weakness. It is a symbol of strength. Humility is key to a successful life.

When you become humble, it helps you make good decisions for everyone. In order to be successful, we must let go of the anger, hatred, egos, and all those negative thoughts that block our vision and our ability to make good choices. As gang members, the anger blocked our vision, causing us to commit violent acts. Maybe it's a bit like the old saying, "Count to ten before you act." We must pause before we react in inappropriate ways.

Beware of roadblocks, and there are many, that deny your understanding of humility. Vanity, smugness, arrogance, envy, domination, snobbery, self-righteousness, and your coolest jackass ways are called pride. At one time, pride was one of your defenses while walking the streets of Chicago. Struttin' down the street or the prison hallway, showing the *shorties* your *mean-muggin' ways*, is nothing but flashing your pride for all to see. It is the culmination of behaviors that hold us back from embracing humility.

Perhaps some words from Jesus can lead the way. *Jesus came to them walking on the water. The fishermen screamed in terror, for they thought he was a ghost. But Jesus immediately spoke to them, reassuring them. "Don't be afraid," he said. "Come along."*

Peter went over to the side of the boat and walked on the water towards Jesus. But when he looked around at the high waves, he was terrified and began to sink. "Save me Jesus Peter shouted."

We share this story to show you that if you believe and stay focused, you can over come anything. But if you pay attention to the lessons learned from the gangs, you will sink. Just look at your life. When you lose focus on your goals, your troubled ways of an earlier life can return.

Discussion Questions for Humility

1) When our ego gets in the way, it becomes difficult to handle a simple problem. How can you find a way to avoid physical confrontation?

2) When a person calls you out, do you want to fight? Do you feel disrespected?

3) What will you do?

    a) talk trash?

    b) fight?

    c) ignore the comment?

    d) address the issue with humility?

    e) all of the above

4) Why do you think that God created humility?

Spirituality

Exploration is the essence of the human spirit.

Frank Borman

Culture is the widening of the mind and of the spirit.

Jawaharlal Nehrue

***

Religion in the hands of bogus people can be a weapon used to manipulate the human mind. Spirituality is the belief that the "self" is found in our spirit or soul. While spirituality teaches us that life on earth is temporary, our spirit is eternal.

Will we be fooled by temptation and materialism, or will we live in harmony with our Creator? Spirituality teaches love of self and others around you, and includes kindness, compassion, justice and a balanced life. While spirituality is not restricted to one religion, it can be said that it is the strength of a deeper spiritual feeling. If our ego and desires control us, then this world will lead to our ruin. Spirituality is about aligning oneself with principles and values in our everyday life; doing what's right when no one is looking.

Traditionally, spirituality is having an attachment to religious values or matters of the spirit, rather than material things. But today, it has taken on to mean higher levels of consciousness using meditation, yoga and similar practices. Zorka Hereford says that being spiritual is when we are in a state of connection with God, Nature, or the deepest part of ourselves.

This is the place where we go to replenish our inner strength needed to accomplish life-changing moments in our lives. Being spiritual removes the controllers of our way of life first imposed upon us through the teachings of prison and street gangs. Spirituality is the pathway for finding the true meaning of life.

Discussion Questions for Spirituality

1) Do you believe God is in your life each and every day? Is God a part of your thinking? Can God help change things?

2) Our spirituality is a part of our moral sense. Spirituality can help build families and create positive role models. How might a sense of spirituality help a gang member to change?

3) If we believe that God created us, then we are his creation. God loves us all. Even our enemies are his creation. God does not want any of us to be controlled by violence and hatred. Do you believe this?

4) Spirituality is to be at peace with yourself and the people around you. How can you express your spirituality to others?

Peace

If we desire a society of peace, then we cannot achieve such a society through violence. If we desire a society without discrimination, then we must not discriminate against anyone in the process of building this society. If we desire a society that is democratic, then democracy must become a means as well as an end.

Bayard Rustin

Islam teaches tolerance, not hatred; universal brotherhood, not enmity; peace, not violence.

Pervez Musharraf

Our most important task is to transform our consciousness so that violence is no longer an option for us in our personal lives; understanding that a world of peace is possible only if we relate to each other as peaceful beings; one individual at a time.

Deepak Chopra

There has to be an inner peace process that treats gang members like traumatized war victims who lack counseling, job, and respect. A lot of that has to be self-administered in affinity groups, counseling groups, in jail and out of jail, with resources and professional help.

Tom Hayden

***

Peace is the perfect flow of the universe and the opposite of war. In prison and in the *'hood*, our minds are hellish, angry, evil, agitated, and looking for the first chance to hurt or kill whoever gets in our way. It is a frame of mind, an inner tranquility that comforts you no matter how bad things become. Peace cannot be achieved in the *'hood* or in our world until we change our value system. When we think like a gang member or thug, *gang'sta* or drug dealer, there is no peace. Instead, there is ego, greed, hopelessness and self-hate. Sooner or later the *'hood* becomes a war zone. And the enemy feeds off the blood, bullets, screams, fear, death, murder and despair. If you want peace, you must have peace in your heart.

In the Menard maximum-security prison built in 1878, Adolfo Davis had no clue as to what it meant to be at peace. His self-imposed hell replaced a peace he never knew. Adolfo needed to experience a stillness in his mind that left room for the peace within his soul. Only then could he expect to reach love and happiness.

Sometimes the simple visualization of an image can be the first step in experiencing the new emotion – peace. Imagine the view of a calm lake, absent of other human activity and the gusty winds of a stormy day. With practice and the passing of time, you can engage in the quiet side of your mind; a place seldom seen by a gang member. Their solitude only comes when they are stoned, unable to make a conscious choice or explore their mental state. Now add to your view the presence of ripples spreading across the surface and the incoming winds that change ripples to waves. To experience peace, we must do so even when we are challenged.

Peace is your fountain of strength; the place you turn to, not only when everything is cool, but also when an outside force challenges you. Peace does not ignore your inner pain or the grief of others. This is an opportunity to drawn upon your strength, the very quality that is leading you to a worthy destination. Each time you sit with peace, you replenish your strength to grow and do even greater things.

It is in the sitting with peace when you can experience something deeply eternal. Call it God, the Spirit, Unconditional love, or something that defies a chosen label. This is where the deepest feelings of love and peace can be found. Words sometimes come up short in describing this "thing without a name." But it is real and can change your life.

***

A Search for Peace

I walked the streets searching for peace,

found a false reality

Now I'm doing life.

In Hell, a place they call home

But God promised,

Not a place like this.

I make it through another night

Heart aches, tears flow, the pain is deep,

Drop to my knees, no relief.

A dingy-dark cell

Searching for peace,

Trapped in Hell.

Adolfo Davis – Menard Maximum Security Prison 2003

Discussion Questions for Peace

1) What can we say to a gang member about peace?

2) What solution and mindset must a person have to secure peace in the 'hood?

3) Is there anyone in the neighborhood to talk with about peace?

4) Can you obtain peace?

5) How can you use social media to speak with friends and foes about peace at school and in the 'hood?

6) What about peace at home? How might peace at home translate into peace on the streets?

7) If you had the power to talk to all of the gangs in your community, what would you say to them?

Forgiveness

While revenge weakens society, forgiveness gives it strength.

Dalai Lama

Let us forgive each other – only then will we live in peace.

Leo Nikolaevich Tolstoy

When you hold resentment toward another, you are bound to that person or condition by an emotional link that is stronger than steel. Forgiveness is the only way to dissolve that link and get free.

Catherine Ponder

For if you forgive men when they sin against you, your heavenly Father will also forgive you. But if you do not forgive men their sins, your Father will not forgive your sins.

Matthew 6: 14-15

***

The opposite of retaliation is forgiveness. How do we forgive another gang member who kills one of your guys? Why not just pick up a gun and handle your *B.I.?* With that kind of thinking, the cycle never stops. When it's all about "an eye for en eye and a tooth for a tooth, only the blind and the toothless will be left."(Gandhi) Forgiveness is about empathy and understanding that a power bigger than us, the Creator, is in control and ultimately punishes and forgives. God is the giver of life and death.

Practicing forgiveness takes you out of the cycle of revenge, payback and retaliation. Forgiveness allows you to let go of all the hate, anger and move on with your life. You may grieve your loss but good judgment comes more quickly than the person pulling the trigger. Forgive, as you want to be forgiven.

It took us a long time to forgive. If someone did something that hurt us, we would retaliate. You never let anyone get the better of you. That's how we were brought up. It took Patrick and Adolfo years to forgive their parents, and the mothers of their children for keeping the children away from us. It was extremely difficult for Stanley to forgive the police who killed his uncle.

Forgiveness is hard, but it's a journey that we all must take. We have to understand the fact that we made bad choices in life and we want forgiveness. But it's just as important, and more so, for us to forgive the ones who hurt us. Letting go of the anger brings us internal peace.

The act of forgiving is necessary for spiritual growth. These feelings of anger, hatred, and resentment sap the strength from your soul. By letting go of these emotions, you will feel a weight removed from your shoulder. Only then can you move forward on your chosen path. There are several chapters in your life's story filled with good and bad guys. Some makeup short scenes in a chapter, and others consume a powerful good or bad influence in your story. Embrace them all for what they are and move forward.

In the beginning it can seem quite difficult, but it is necessary to connect to your Spirit. This will take time through your quite thoughts, meditation, and prayer. You must sit with your thoughts in order to understand their significance in your life. Let the goodness, the love, and the feeling of wellbeing flow through your body like a gentle river. After some experimentation on your part, you will feel the positive flow of emotions. Forgiveness will follow. In time, others will sense the positive change in you and will want to be part of your life.

It's during our sleeping hours that our body replenishes itself with energy. Sleep provides the opportunity for our soul to be filled with love and positive thoughts. Never go to sleep with negative thoughts or they will most likely be reinforced throughout the night. Think about filling your soul with love and the glory of God. That is how your spirit grows. The act of forgiveness will follow. Some of our most outstanding artists, spiritual leaders, philosophers, and any who aspire to growth, will use their sleep hours to replenish their soul, and find new discoveries that improve their life.

Switch the focus of blaming others to understanding yourself. Allow the experience of sitting with yourself to unfold. Rather than blaming others, allow yourself to understand your part in any misunderstanding. Be open. Be cool. That is a measure of strength.

Discussion Questions for Forgiveness

1) While growing up we might have heard words like, "I hate you. You are not my brother or sister." Later on when something happens that hurts us, we might not want to forgive those in our family. How can we work towards forgiveness?

2) Forgiveness starts with each of us, and must come with peace and the act of humbling ourselves. Without either of these two things, wanting peace and humility, forgiveness is shallow at best. How might I begin the process of forgiving?

3) Have you ever tried to forgive an enemy? Have you ever tried to forgive yourself?

4) The world doesn't teach us to forgive and is often times a very unforgiving place. Does this mean that forgiveness is not possible?

Compassion

Love and compassion are necessities, not luxuries. Without them humanity cannot survive.

Dalai Lama

In the crowd, herd, or gang, it is a mass-mind that operates – which is to say, a mind without subtlety, a mind without compassion, a mind, finally, uncivilized.

Robert Lindner

If your compassion does not include yourself, it is incomplete.

Buddha

***

Everything in the *'hood* comes down to control through violence or fear of violence. While brutality often starts in the home and moves to the block, gangs use violations to control their own. Violence is everywhere. That might be all you've ever known. But it doesn't have to be that way. Compassion and empathy (trying to understand what the other person is going through) enable us to better understand another person instead of wanting to knock his grill out when he messes up.

People do dumb stuff all of the time. Only when we recognize that we all make mistakes, can we learn compassion, forgiveness and have empathy for others. In the *'hood*, people would rather be feared than loved. But they end up consumed by lies or killed by others. Compassionate people help others, and in the process, help themselves.

Living in a violent world can sometimes leave little room for compassion. So how can we learn to have compassion when we have never been exposed to the art of loving, caring, and having empathy for others? The first step is to master the art of listening. Have you ever noticed how much easier it is to talk than listen to another person? Listening can be exhaustive. You must be open minded and willing to consider the other person's thoughts. Never be judgmental during the conversation. The other person will sense your lack of interest and turn away. Respond to his/her emotion, not to his words. Remember the whole person. He might have some qualities you dislike, but there might be other characteristics that you can support. Try to imagine yourself in the other person's shoes. This too can help.

It is very important to develop a support system of like-minded people who, like yourself, are pursuing the path of love and happiness. Sharing experiences, gains and failures, frustrations, and moments of joy benefits everyone in your group. Working together towards common goals adds strength and courage to all members.

Discussion Questions for Compassion

1) If there was more compassion in society, would there still be a lot of crime?

2) Does showing compassion make you appear weak?

3) If compassion had been in the home of gang bangers while they were growing up, do you think they would have joined the gang?

4) How do you feel about people that are different than you? Can you have compassion for them?

Legit Hustle

If you have an idea of what you want to do in your future, you must go at it with almost monastic obsession, be it music, the ballet or just a basic degree. You have to go at it single-mindedly and let nothing get in your way.

Henry Rollins

***

Hustle is doing anything you need to do to make money. If you make money, you hustle. Legit hustle is taking that same drive, ambition, and determination and making it work while following the rule of law. Some might say that hustle is all consuming, like your past addiction for criminal activity. Remember the rush you felt? You can experience the same when you succeed in your chosen occupation.

They say it's the land of the free but ain't nothing free and that's why hustling is in our genes. The experience we get selling drugs, *cop*, and *flip* can be taken to the legal format where it's all about copping and flipping in our business.

Trust me. The Creator gave us all the skills to pay the bills and this is a gift. All you have to do is know yourself and find your skill set; learn the rules to that industry and most of all, educate yourself. I'm not talking about some dead end job even though you might have to do the 9 to 5 thing for a while, and there ain't nothing wrong with that. I'm talking about having a career and using your God-given talent. A job is something you do but a career is something you live to do. The rappers tell us that there is a short cut to the top and while chasing fast cash we get *dropped or popped*. However, true success takes thinking, planning, education and work – lots of work. When you figure that out, everything you are meant to have, you will get.

Set your goal, master your plan. You can do it with the Lord's helping hand. Imagine that you have set the goal of climbing Mount Everest, one of the highest mountains in the world, located on the border of Nepal and Tibet. What would be needed to master your climb? The most obvious asset would be the physical skills, technique, experience, and strength. In addition you need numerous items such as a backpack, ice axe, 12-point crampons, helmet, climbing harness with belay loop, 3 locking carabiners, oxygen bottles, sleep bag, proper clothing, and some 20 additional pieces of equipment.

Next would be the grand plan needed to accomplish your objective. Perhaps the most important asset might be your determination, passion, drive, ambition, and if I can use one word – "hustle." While climbing Mount Everest is a huge challenge unattainable by most men, changing your life requires the ultimate "hustle." Master the steps and you will reap what you sow.

Discussion Questions for Legit Hustle

1) A legit hustle does not have to be a hard thing to do. It can be a commitment to reach a promising goal but requires discipline and sacrifice on your part. Education is the tool that enables you to succeed. Staying in school allows you to become someone with a legit hustle. Think about what you would like to become someday and write about it in 3 paragraphs or more.

2) Once you have your goals, how can you stay committed to them? How can you get past the temptations to do other things instead?

3) Do you believe your goals are worth more than nice clothes, shoes, and other material things?

Unity

We must all hang together, or assuredly we shall all hang separately.

Benjamin Franklin

Make my joy complete by being of the same mind, maintaining the same love, united in spirit, intent on one purpose.

Philippians 4:2

We come to reason, not to dominate. We do not seek to have our way, but to find a common way.

Lyndon B. Johnson

Bringing the gifts that my ancestors gave. I am the dream and the hope of the slave. I rise, I rise, I rise.

Maya Angelou

Unity is strength.

Division is weakness.

African Proverb

***

The opposite of division is unity, our nation's greatest strength. Today, the gang structure has been smashed to bits and all the pieces that remain are fighting for crumbs and dying with none. When we finally stop hating each other and realize that the culture of death in the streets is dragging us all to hell, we can evolve into a life with our Creator and the life he intended for us.

Unity will bring us to a new era of cooperation where you want the same for your brother/sister that you want for yourself. Through a group of two or more people we find the collective strength in unity. Your group can be your immediate family, former gang members, like-minded inmates, or any group with agreed upon objectives. Everyone must be on the same page, wanting to achieve the shared goals. Talk with your group and determine what goals you agree upon. Only then can you experience the strength found in Unity.

It's easy to mistakenly think that your group might resemble street or prison gangs. But that is far from the truth. Your chosen group would not have any of the characteristics found in your former gangs. The drugs, violence, brain washing, destruction, false love, zero compassion and understanding, are traits found in your former gangs. No, this is your group that shares the respectable goals that will change your life and bring you to a place of love and happiness.

Discussion Questions for Unity

A nation united is a very powerful political and economical force. A divided nation will be destroyed. What does unity mean to you when it comes to your ethnic heritage? Your community? Your school? Your home?

Answer with a one page essay.

Communication

To effectively communicate, we must realize that we are all different in the way we perceive the world and use this understanding as a guide to our communication with others.

Tony Robbins

Precision of communication is important, more important than ever, in our era of hair trigger balances, when a false or misunderstood word may create as much disaster as a sudden thoughtless act.

James Thurber

The less people know, the more they yell.

Seth Godin

Communication – the human connection – is the key to personal and career success.

Paul J. Meyer

***

After we decide to break from our destructive life style of isolation and find ourselves still alive, there is hope. We need to move from isolation to communication with our family, and say to ourselves, "I want to change. I want to put my life on the straight path of redemption and forgiveness."

First, we think it, say it, then act on it; thought, word and action. People and opportunities will come into our life. It isn't easy and our word will be tested. There will be the doubters. But as Matthew 12:33 states, *"Make a tree good and its fruit will be good, or make a tree bad and its fruit will be bad, for a tree is recognized by its fruit."*

Communication is using all of the change steps we have discussed in this book. We cannot communicate effectively with our peers without experiencing love, empathy, humility, peace, forgiveness, compassion, and the other skills we have discussed. Only when they are combined can we communicate our desires and goals with other people.

Discussion Questions for Communication

1) What does communication mean to you?

2) What does it mean to be a good communicator?

3) What are the tools necessary to be an affective communicator?

Destination

Love is our true destiny. We do not find the meaning of life by ourselves alone – We find it with another.

Thomas Merton

What lies behind us and what lies before us are tiny matters compared to what lies within us.

Ralph Waldo Emerson

***

No matter where we've been, we can overcome our past. But if we refuse to change and continue our criminal behavior, our destination will become worse than before. If, however, you connect with your Creator and the life you have been given, your spirit will lead you through your journey. While it won't be easy, weaker people have completed the journey and made contributions to our society. Make your family proud.

While it is easy to say that we want a better life, we must focus on the journey that leads us to the desired destination. It is a common mistake for people to focus more on the destination rather than the journey. We sometimes long for the projected goal, instead of accepting where we are and move forward. Worrying too much on reaching your destination can lead to elevated stress and unhappiness Know where you are going but focus on the steps you must take in order to fulfill your objective.

Progress requires patience. Sometimes it takes longer than you think to reach your goal. And that's okay. Think about the steps you've agreed to take – love, empathy, education, humility, spirituality, peace, forgiveness, compassion, unity, communication. Sometimes people will keep a personal journal, recording daily improvements and setbacks. By doing so, you maintain the focus on the small steps leading to your predetermined destination. When pursuing a personal goal, you become excited about where your path might lead. While it's natural, don't let your enthusiasm for the destination block out your daily progress. Remember, it's one step after another.

Discussion Questions for Destination

1) What is your destination?

2) Do you think your happiness depends on where you are going?

3) Do you think your children's future is dependent on you?

4) Your destination will be the result of education and self-knowledge, or the lack of it.

Chicago Gangs

Chicago Gangs: Then & Now

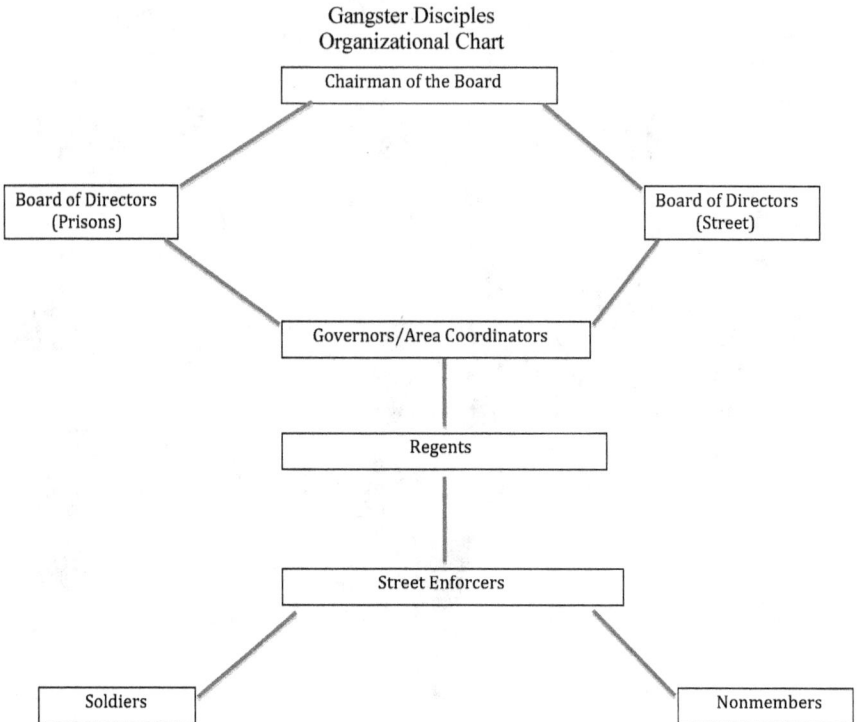

Gangster Disciples
Organizational Chart

Chairman of the Board

Board of Directors
(Prisons)

Board of Directors
(Street)

Governors/Area Coordinators

Regents

Street Enforcers

Soldiers

Nonmembers

It is an undeniable fact of life that gangs and their attendant activities have always been and will continue to be an inseparable part of the social dynamics that establishes and maintains the only true semblance of the prison's order and the relative peace. . . . In the midst of a severe austere prison environment that is charged with the potential for violence at any given moment the lone individual is vulnerable. . . . One's safety in prison is a tenuous proposition at best. On the bottom line, survival becomes the paramount pre-occupation, your well being is a matter of constant concern, the only reality one can count on is right now, the present, this moment, tomorrow is fraught with uncertainty.
Larry "King" Hoover, leader of the Gangster Disciples, spoke of the importance of prison gangs in a letter to his parole board in 1993.

Prior to the 21st century, structure, discipline, leadership, protection, drugs, money, and the perception of the gang as a family unit, contributed to the unity of the Chicago gang. Strong leadership was needed and could be seen in the organizational structure of the Gangster Disciples led by Larry "King" Hoover from the 1960's through the 90's. Each level of leadership played their part in carrying out the goals of the gang – sell drugs, guns, prostitution, protection, friendships, guns, to name a few. A gang member was able to provide the basics – food, shelter and money -- for themselves and family. It was a tried and proven way of gang members to survive in and out of a prison setting. Take away the leadership from the top and the gang began to splinter into small out-of-control groups.

According to the old-time Chicago gang members, the idea was to generate revenue for the nation through drug sales. To do so meant that the gang should avoid police scrutiny that came with violent crimes. Junior members were told not to settle disagreements with gunfire unless they had permission from their elders. Accountability and consequences were key words. Each member had to be responsible for their actions or prepared to suffer the consequences.

The gang killings today, unlike the gangs of Hoover's days, are less about money and more about reputation, disrespect, revenge, and robbery. Accumulating money for the gang/nation is not what today's gangs are all about.

Many stories have been, and will continue to be written about Chicago gangs, then and now. They all share the common belief that the lack of leadership in today's gangs has increased street violence. On February 17, 2017, Michael Tobin authored *Chicago Gang members say more police won't stop the murders* for <u>Fox News Channel, FNC.</u> Based on Tobin's interviews, law enforcement made a bad situation worse. It was their belief that removal of the gang leaders would diminish gang violence. As Gangster Tony Cannon said, "Ain't like it used to be. Back then we had structure. Older guy would make us go to school. Even though we was gang banging, we would still go to school."

The removal of gang leaders has not experienced the positive affects law enforcement had intended. While the gangs remain powerful, they function much like a rudderless boat – out of control and without direction. According to Michael Tobin, young gang members try to gain respect by being ruthless. Getting a certain number of kills or hurting people they once feared proves their toughness. One former gang member claims that kids want nice clothes, fast money and how many kills they can get. That's what many of the gangsters on the streets of Chicago want.

Despite the increased violence, a member of the Black Disciples said the gang is all that he's been able to count on. "I live by this gun and I live by these drugs, this product that I'm selling, and I'm pushing in this neighborhood. It's putting food on my table and food in my kids' mouths and a roof over their heads, then I'm not going to put it down." Others say the violent gang life is for kids. If they live to their mid 20s and stay out of jail, they have a slim chance to walk away and find a job.

Stamp Corbin wrote *The Chicago Gang Diaspora and the Orgin of Gun Violence,* 12-06-17, Huffington Post. The root of the problem is the Chicago gang displacement. The closing of the housing projects and the haste to relocate the residents created a major problem. One such housing project was Cabrini-Greene that housed 15,000 residents. Like other housing projects, Cabrini-Greene was known for crime, drugs, violence and gangs.

The project had a dividing line with different gangs on the north and south sides of Division Street. When it was closed, families were moved to other housing projects or used housing vouchers to locate in the West and South sides of Chicago. The relocation of residents did not consider the gang affiliation of each family. As a result, gangs that were divided by Division Street in Cabrini-Green now lived next to each other in new neighborhoods, leading to shootings across the entire city on the West and South sides. Corbin believes that a generation will be lost until there is a realignment of gang location.

In 2017, there were 3,561 shootings (651 murdered) in Chicago. That's what happens when gang leaders and members don't understand where their territory begins and ends.

The only solution is to reevaluate each family and house them in neighborhoods with similar cultural backgrounds. While it may sound a bit far-fetched, Corbin believes it will save lives.

Throughout gang history, the weapons of choice have changed. Decades ago gang members used clubs, baseball bats, rocks, chains, and the occasional six-shooter as their weapon. When the confrontation ended, there were broken bones, blood spilled, hurt feelings, and the rare killing by a handgun. But in the 21st century, firepower has increased the killings to unimaginable numbers.

Gangs have moved to the semi-automatic handguns with extended magazines holding as many as 30 rounds. Instead of the sporadic bang bang of the six-shooting revolver, the sound heard throughout the neighborhood has been replaced by the rapid sound of semi-automatic weapons. Now the AK-15s and AK-47s, military semi-automatic assault rifles, have been added to their arsenal. The rifle offers increased accuracy, a 30-round magazine, more velocity and power, and a shooting distance up to 650 yards. A city block is 220 yards.

A common shooting with the assault rifle is to have a scout car locate the target, followed by a second car or van carrying the rifles that spray the air with destructive .223-caliber bullets. Since the rifle penetrates standard-issue bulletproof vests, the policemen experience greater risk. Imagine the risk an officer would feel as he walked down a darkened alley or an unlit abandoned building.

When Adolfo Davis joined a gang in the 1980's, there was structure within the nation (gang). There were laws/policies that governed us, and if we broke these rules, we would be punished. The fear of being violated, kept everyone on his square. There were two rules that stood out the most. No member should do any drugs that are addictive. When you are hooked on drugs, you will do anything that supports your habit. That can sometimes lead to stealing money and drugs from the nation. And that was not tolerated.

My best friend, age 16, was getting high on cocaine and stealing money to pay for his drugs. He was caught taking money from the nation. Their response was to tie him to a tree and beat him while we watched. They showed us what happens when you steal money from the gang. The beating changed my friend forever. He was physically and mentally traumatized to the point where he seemed like a different person. In a few years he was killed. To this day, most of us who witnessed that beating don't take addictive drugs.

The second rule is that you don't bring on the "heat." When you bring the police to the hood it stops the flow of money and gets people locked up. Even if you got locked up in the cook county jail or went to prison, you were still subject to punishment. And if you went to juvy, they waited until you got out. The nation took pride in holding members accountable for breaking their rules. There were even a few moral laws and policies we honored – don't sell drugs to kids or pregnant women. And if you got locked up for rape or for something sick, you paid the price.

When Adolfo Davis became a gang member, the rules provided structure and meaning to the nation.

Unity – We stood together, and when we went anywhere the rules were to be accepted.

Respect – We respected both our fellow members and other gangs.

Love – Although it was a "false" love, we loved each other.

Family – We belonged to a group, a family.

Trust – It was important to trust each other. Without trust, we could never be a family.

Honor – We didn't move without vision. We stood with honor.

Accountability – Each gang member was held accountable for his actions.

Fear – This is what kept you in check.

We went to "gang school" where we learned all of the laws and policies. If you didn't, you were punished. Following the rules kept you safe and maintained your presence in the nation.

In 1995, everything changed. The FBI began taking down my gang, the Gangster Disciples, and other Chicago street gangs as well. Once the Feds locked up the gang leaders and chiefs, we lost the glue that held us together. Gangs began to lose their structure. Those of us who were locked up tried to hold on, but the gang leaders told us to chill out so they could go home. When they were eventually released and returned to the hood they said, "fuck you." While we felt abandon, the laws and policies were still part of us. Many of the gang members in prison sacrificed their lives for the nation and will never see freedom again. All they have left are memories of the gang they called family.

But those kids in the outside world were worst off than us. They didn't have the laws and policies, and the structure to hold them together. They were left to fight for themselves. They lacked direction. When the Feds took down the gangs, they created something far worse.

In December of 2014, Adolfo was transferred to the Cook county jail where his original life sentence was vacated. Three months later, in March of 2015, a hearing was held where the judge resentenced Adolfo to life without parole. In 2017, while living in the Stateville maximum-security prison, Adolfo's life without parole sentence was vacated for a second time, and he was awarded a new sentence of 60 years, 30 years for good behavior. His parole date was moved to December 31, 2020.

The court hearing was the result of a 2012 Supreme Court ruling, *Miller v. Alabama,* stating that juveniles could not be sentenced to life without parole because their brains were not fully developed at such a young age. Illinois inmates who fit that description received a new sentencing hearing for their past crimes.

It was in the Cook county jail where the young gang members made an immediate impression upon Adolfo. "I've watched the news and read newspapers and I even spoke with many of them when they came to prison. But in the county jail they were straight off the streets, raw and uncut."

Ninety percent of the guys on each deck were addicted to street drugs or medications, and maintained a constant "high." According to Adolfo, the young gangsters didn't care about nothing. "It broke my heart. So I asked those who were approachable, "Why is it so crazy on the streets?"

"We doing what we have to do to survive and its better than you," was their answer. They felt like the older gang members had abandoned them and the nation. They have this built in hate for those before them. They said that if any old timer gets out and tries to come to the hood and change things, he's going to get killed.

Adolfo knew some old timers who got out of prison and tried to bring structure back to the nation. They were killed. The young ones said that they like how it is, and they don't want to hear from the members who came before them.

What I saw in those kids' eyes was nothing. Most of the time it was a blank stare. This generation has no structure, no fear, and no laws or policies to hold them together. They don't trust or respect anyone. There is no unity. They even kill, rob and hurt people in their own gang. They are addicts. The structure, false sense of love, family, belonging, and accountability are not there. The laws and policies that brought order are gone, and from that came *The Urban Street Terrorist.*

***

Seven people, including 4 men killed in a gang-retaliation attack at a fast-food restaurant, and a pregnant woman with a gunshot wound to her head, were gunned down Thursday in three separate incidents within blocks of each other.

A 27-year old man and a 23-year old woman were fatally shot as they drove near the South Shore Cultural Center on Thursday. The woman sitting in the front passenger seat, suffered a gunshot wound to the head, and the man – a documented gang member – was shot in the side. Both were pronounced dead at the scene.
As reported by Aamer Madhani, *Chicago Violence: 7 killed in 1 neighborhood in 12 hours*, 3-31-17 USA Today

***

A pregnant woman was among four people shot to death in Brighton Park; a bloodbath stemming from an ongoing gang war in the Southwest Side of Chicago. They all suffered multiple gunshot wounds. Dozens of gold rifle casings littered the street and sidewalk nearby. Marisela Rodriogues said she was putting away the dishes in her apartment some three blocks away when she heard rapid gunfire. "It sounded like something our of a movie," she said

As reported by Taylor Hartz and Nader Issa, *Pregnant Woman among 4 killed in Brighton Park gang shooting*, 9-16-17, Chicago News

***

Ten people were shot, two fatally, in an act of gang violence in Chicago. The shooting victims had been taking part in a memorial for another person killed in a gang-related murder in the same neighborhood earlier in the day. Two people came out of an alleyway and opened fire with assault rifles on the service that was being held in Brighton Park.

As reported by Chuck Johnson and Susannah Cullinane, *10 shot, 2 killed in 'brazen' Chicago gang shooting*, 5-07-17, CNN

***

A July 4th weekend in 2017 turned a holiday into a bloody bath on the streets of Chicago. One-hundred-and-two people were shot with 15 fatalities. The shootings happened on the South and West sides of Chicago.

"You just destroyed somebody's family," one of the victim's relatives said. His uncle was fatally shot in front of his home, with children narrowly escaping gunfire. A car came racing through the alley, shooting. "My mom could have got killed," a bystander said. "My auntie's kids could have got killed. They don't care."

Gordon was dropping two young cousins at a relative's home when police said gunfire erupted in an apartment building parking lot. A bullet intended for someone in another vehicle hit Gordon in the face while he sat in his car two parking spots away. The gunfire barely missed his 6-year-old and 8-year-old cousins, who were sitting in the back seat. Detectives believe several of the shootings were motivated by gang

retaliation, and alcohol was a factor in many others. Another holiday weekend on the
streets of Chicago where the rapid fire of bullets pierced the dark-black nights.
As reported by Jessica D'Onofrio, Leah Hope, and Eric Homg, *102 shot, 15 fatalities, in*
Chicago over July 4 holiday weekend, 7-05-17, <u>WLS News.</u>

While the Chicago gangs retain their original names adopted many years ago, they
have evolved into a younger, less structured organization. The gangs of the 80s, 90s, and
years before, were run by older leaders with the sole purpose of serving the *nation*, the
organization, the gang. All of the money earned from their criminal activities went to the
nation, to be paid to members as directed by the elders. Some observers believe the
organizational structure of the gangs during the Larry "King" Hoover days, mimicked
Fortune 500 companies. While the criminal activities were not to be admired, the
structure and discipline of the gangs were impressive. But now in the 21st century, many
of the older gang members are in prison, dead, or have chosen a different path.

The gangs of today are younger, less structured and certainly more violent. And
society lacks an agreed upon strategy for reducing their criminal ways. There is the law
enforcement side with an emphasis on punishments, and the more humanistic approach
that centers on each human being with an emphasis on behavior modification. There are
examples where the latter approach has experienced some remarkable success.

Chicago Gang, Prison, and a Better Life

Multiple years or a life sentence in prison can be viewed as hell for eternity. But there is a path for the freedom of your soul. While we never know what the future might bring – will you be released from prison or will it become your place to die – hope can be seen through the sunrise of a beautiful day. View your body and soul as a temple of holiness; reject lessons learned in the early years of your life; and take charge of who you are and who you might be.

During the first part of this book we discussed the lessons learned through gang indoctrination, and the path that led to "death or a prison cell." We then discussed "rebirth" and the way to a different and better life. Yes, there is hope that is dependent upon the choices you are about to take. "Chicago gangs, then and now" is aimed at the youth on the streets or those entering prison; the old-timer looking for a better understanding of his life journey; and to parents and lay persons seeking answers as to why we have such violence on the city streets.

We conclude our discussion by examining the choices – "Chicago Gang, Prison, or a Better Life" – that face many of you in your daily life. Choices can be difficult, especially when the gang is all you know. You don't have to be poor, come from a broken home or a single parent home for this cycle to trap you. It has no mercy, no color preference, age limit, or a gender preference. It's out to destroy you. To better understand the path you might take, we have interviewed several inmates who are currently serving time in the Illinois Department of Corrections. Many chose not to share their feelings due to peer pressure, perhaps personal privacy, the probability that they have not considered the existence of another path, or the belief that this is all bull shit. Some willing to be interviewed are young men entering incarceration. Many are old-timers who have the luxury of thinking, meditating, and praying for a more meaningful life.

***

Michael S. Carlos, Incarcerated 09-02-93, Murder, Aggravated Battery, Life without parole

I am 43 years old and have been incarcerated for 25 years. I grew up in Bloomington, Illinois in a stable environment; both father and mother was present. I have one sibling – brother – who is older.

Growing up in Bloomington, Illinois often found myself looking at the fast street life – drug dealers, hustlers, the movers and the shakers. They had the money and nice cars. Although it was all criminal activity they were involved in, that life excited me and I wanted to taste that life.

My father and mother was both the 6 am to 5 pm type people, work hard everyday, made sure a roof stayed over our head and even though we didn't have much we never wanted for nothing nor went without. "Pops" is a Baptist preacher and my mother, well, she is the "first lady."

I remember in 1984 my brother came home. I was 10 years old, he was 13 or 14 years old and he had joined a gang, the Gangster Disciples. It was fascinating to me, even the fact that he was all bruised up because he was "jumped in," beat up, and I wanted to follow in his footsteps.

Fast forward 4 years and now I am part of the same gang and I was the embodiment of this gang – the do whatever type, drug dealing, guns, hustling, gangbanging. Never did I use drugs due to that being prohibited by the laws and policies of the gang. That fast life 4 year later ended me up in jail on the charges of 8 counts of first degree murder, two people were shot and killed. I was 18 years old and was given a natural life without parole sentence.

Imagine navigating your way through a life at 19 years old in Stateville's Maximum-security prison in Joliet, Illinois, the worst of the worst, and the baddest of the bad are there. I told myself that I was going to survive by any means necessary, therefore I acted just as crazy as they did and that crap actually worked. They assumed I was heartless too.

I wasn't known to be a trouble maker but was known to be able to hold my own in any situation. The older men there would say to me that because of the way I articulate myself that I would move up in the ranks of the gang fast due to me being able to reach anyone no matter what level or educational background and they were right. But I always knew this person that everyone seen was not who I was nor who god intended for me to be.

Ten years later I was 29 years old, and still in the thick of things. I had been transferred to another maximum-security prison down state 4 years prior. I was in segregation for most of my stay at that prison due to gang activities or investigations concerning same.

What people mean for bad, God means for good. At 35 years old, now back at Stateville, I found myself at the fork in the road of life. Do I continue to spiral out of control or do I let go and let God?

To choose to walk away from the gang, no strings attached. This was a very hard decision to make especially inside these walls. In all actuality I was lost without the gang. It had been my identity for so long. A lot of my peers felt as though I had abandoned our struggle.

My faith is what got me through that period. I went back to the core foundation of who I am – the essence of God. We are created in the image and likeness of Him. I knew that it was so easy to do what is wrong but so very difficult to do what is right. I had chosen the spiritual path of Islam. I remember the first time I made Salah (Prayer). I knew at the moment that this is what I'm suppose to be doing, submitting my will to the will of God. I'm not some religious fanatic but I understand the life I was leading was wrong and I believe the path that I am on will not only uplift myself but bring others into the light of themselves by my example.

I also engulfed myself in programs to re-educate the mind to spark the change within me and plant the seeds within others. Rehabilitation became my focus along with re-learning who I am and what my purpose is here while incarcerated. I have completed many programs within the facility, DePaul and Northwestern universities inside and out student exchange Restorative Justice programs and some restorative programs through the mail

The change within me caused the maximum institution to have me transferred to a medium facility where I am still continuing to move in positive directions in showing the young men here that I am your example. If I can change and I'm just like you, you can too.

"Illinois Constitution Article 1, section 11" states, "That all penalties shall be determined both according to the seriousness of the offense and with the objective of restoring the offender to useful citizenship" Due to recent U.S. Supreme court rulings, my case is back in the courts with hopes of getting the sentence reduced to give me a second chance at life.

***

Adolfo Davis, AKA Spoon Cake, Holy Name Wali (Loyal Friend), Projected Parole Date – 12-31-2020

I was charged with 2 First Degree Murders, 2 Attempted Murders, and Home Invasion; sentenced to life without parole. The south side of Chicago was home until my incarceration at age 14. My family lived in my grandmother's one-room cellar apartment. I have 9 siblings, 8 on my father's side and 1 on my mother's. There was my crack-addicted mother, an absentee father, my grandmother's bed-ridden husband, her mentally disabled son, and a bunch of other grandchildren living in the room.

There was lots of pressure to join a gang. Lots of my friends had older brothers who were members of the Gangster Disciples, a Chicago gang. One day they asked us if we would be interested in making $250. per week to watch out for the police. We said yes, and we were members of the Gangster Disciples just like that.

While I made bad grades in school, I wanted to learn. Other kids made fun of me because of my clothes were old and bad. So I started beating people up to keep them from making fun of me. But when I joined the gang I wasn't going to school anyways, and I was no longer wearing old, bad clothes.

The emotional pain from not having parents who love you is terrible. If I allowed myself to think about my situation, I thought about suicide. When I was 12, I played Russian Roulette, and tried to hang myself in the Audy juvenile home. But the ceiling didn't hold my weight.

In 1998, when I spent fours years in the Tamms supermax prison, I was isolated in a single cell with fewer distractions than I had in the maximum-security prisons. This caused me to think about myself and what I wanted my life to be. And then I made a life-changing decision to work with a psychologist at Tamms. She helped me to evaluate my past decisions and the future ones that I needed to consider. After 4 years of therapy, I was transferred back to the maximum-security prison where I could visit family members.

I had no choice but to change if I wanted a better life for myself and for the people that I love. Tired of living in a false sense of reality that only causes destruction, pain, and sadness. I long for freedom, marriage, success, and to help rebuild my community. I believe in myself, that I will succeed in what I set out to do. Since my days in the supermax prison, I have implemented the steps for rebirth as outlined in this book.

***

Frank Felder AKA China Man, Incarcerated 07-12-96, Projected Discharge – Ineligible

I was incarcerated in 1992 for attempted murder and robbery, and sentenced to life in prison without the possibility of parole. I lived in the Westside of Chicago with my mother, and visited my father frequently. While my father never came to visit, I would go to see him.

My mother worked for a shipping company plus she was a hustler, a drug dealer. My father was a straight hustler, that's all he did was sell dope. I have 2 siblings on my mother's side, and 4 on my father's.

The Vice Lord nation was a gang in my neighbor. My older brother was a member and I liked the support I got from them and what I saw. It was in the Vice Lord gang when the police arrested me for carrying a gun case. I spent a short amount of time in juvenile detention. I was kicked out of high school for participating in a fight between the Vice Lord and the Satan disciples. I was moved to an alternate school to get my G.E.D. But that was soon closed. Then I went to a job core in Indiana and completed my G.E.D. I also learned carpentry, building, and maintenance skills. At the job core, I helped set up the structuring of the Vice Lord nation.

After the job core was complete, I moved by to the Westside of Chicago and began working with my mother at a shipping company. I felt like I had my life in order. I was making some money and had a steady job. But when I lost my job, I went down hill from there. I went deeper into gang life and started doing some serious hustling. I stayed with the Vice Lord gang because they were my family.

After I was sent to prison, I began to make a change in my life at age 29. It was then that I walked away from the gang. While some members were not happy with me, others looked at me as a role model of what to do to have some success in a dark place. The first step I took to begin my change was to start listening. This is the key to living life in prison.

Everyday I will continue to grow mentally, spiritually, and emotionally, and set an example for the men around me. I dream about getting out of prison, helping my family and my children. My message is to put God first, mean it, believe it and live it.

***

Marvin Williford, Incarcerated 10-26-04, First Degree Murder, Parole Date 02-08-2083

I am 46 years old and have been incarcerated for nearly 15 years, serving an 80-year sentence for murder, armed robbery, and armed violence. One of the many things that my incarceration has taught me is the value of self-inventory and reflection.

Growing up, I lived in a two-parent household with three older brothers. My father worked at a factory for nearly forty years and my mother worked various jobs from being a cashier to working at a local hospital in its cafeteria. Our home was filled with love and my parents made sure that we have the essentials to not only survive, but to prosper as well. My parents and older brothers provided me with living examples of manhood, hard work, and dedication while at home. But outside of my door was a totally different environment that would eventually consume me to some degree.

As a youngster growing up on the west-side of Chicago, decisions and choices didn't seem all that important to me. You lived for today, not tomorrow. Unfortunately, it was just "normal" to step out of your door to a world that was filled with gang banging, drug dealing, prostitution, and everything else that came with it. I was a church kid who went to church every Sunday, sang in the choir, and was even a junior deacon at one point. I can remember "ducking down" in the back seat of my dad's old car as he drove us home from church through the neighborhood. I was embarrassed to be seen with my church *clothes on and I would run as fast as I could from the car to the door of our house so nobody would see me. As I grew older, I pulled away from my family structure and spiritual foundation. I became enamored with the streets. Why work at some factory job that pays me $300 per week, when I can make that in one day selling rocks? Working a "9 to 5" seemed like a suck-a-move to me.*

The Gangster Disciples ran the neighborhood that I grew up in and their chief ran things with an iron fist. Fear was attached to his name due to his reputation in the streets, but he also wouldn't allow any of this members to "serve' in the middle of the blocks out of respect to the adults who worked all week and so that the kids could play in some sort of peace. Gang members carried old women's grocery bags to the women's apartments and homes.

But it was a Vice Lord, nicknamed"Blue," who grabbed my attention back then. Even though he was a member of the Gangster Disciples rival gang, he still came through the neighborhood each day to visit his girlfriend who lived on my block. He not only had the finest girl in our neighborhood he also wore the latest gear and the biggest of jewelry I'd ever seen. To top it off, he drove one of the baddest trucks in the land. You would hear him before you saw him because he had one of the loudest sound systems in the area. I idolized him and wanted to mimic his every move.

It wasn't long before Blue had a beef with the chief of the Gangster Disciples and when the dust cleared, both men remained. But Blue had cemented himself in our neighborhood as being certified because he went toe to toe with a legend. For me, that was it. I sat my Bible down and picked-up a "job" and went to work for Blue. Blue was not only a man to be feared, but also one to be respected in the streets, and I was proud to be in his presence along with his soldiers. Between what I saw each and everyday in my neighborhood along with the images that I absorbed from television movies, and music videos, I felt as if I was living the life. It wasn't long before Blue was snatched up on a murder case and sentenced to 60 plus years in prison.

After seeing what happened to Blue and his comrades concerning long prison sentences, I tried to work a regular 9 to 5 for a while but that didn't work for me. I began selling whatever I could. Cocaine, heroin, weed, guns, ammo, and even Viagra pills for $25 a pop. I moved cocaine from Chicago to other nearby states while setting up weed spots in the smaller towns. It wasn't long before I had out-of-towners coming to the city to purchase what they thought was cocaine, but in reality was "dummy-work." You could take a few good ounces of cocaine to the right person and then he'd "blow them up" with garbage to make it appear as if it was a full kilo of cocaine.

Robbing dope dealers was profitable, but dangerous. I didn't think about prison, I was more interested in the money. To be honest, as stupid as this may sound, I used to dream about going to prison. As sick as that statement is, it was the truth for me back then. In most urban-ghettos in the United States, prison was often looked at as a rite of passage for young black and brown males. I didn't want to go for a long time, just six-months or so to see what it was really like. Then I'd come home to this big party, picnic, and celebration. My street credentials would raise a few notches and people would know my name.

Nobody celebrated valedictorians in the hood. Nobody praised you for being good at science or math. If you were book smart, you tried to hide that fact because you would be looked upon as goofy or a nerd. That's why today I have the most respect for those youths out there who wear their intelligence like a medal and those who are brave enough to not buy into the hype of the streets. Back then prison wasn't a stigma that you shunned, you embraced it and in most circles, you were respected because of it.

I have been shot at several times and had a pistol put to my head with the threat of death, but it was one particular situation that caused me to rethink my life. A guy who was no more than 15 to 20 feet away from us was shooting at me and a couple of friends. One of my friends hollered that he was hit and I threw one of his arms over my shoulder and with the help of my other friend, we guided him to an awaiting car. My other buddy jumped into a different car and pulled off. I left as well. The next day I found out that both guys had been shot, one multiple times. But what made me think was, how did the guy behind me get shot multiple times, but I didn't get hit once? I had been shot at before, but this time was different. I couldn't help but to believe that God was showing me that I had a purpose on this earth. When I look back on it now, I know that it was God who was attempting to grab my attention, yet I didn't completely change my ways.

It wasn't until I came to Stateville maximum-security prison that I began to evaluate my life. One of the hardest things that I've had to do was to look at myself in the mirror and be honest with myself regarding my life, my strengths, weaknesses, and just as important, my wasted potential. I've learned at lot from some of the inmates around me.

Since educational programs were pretty none-existent at the time, I was part of a group of guys who formed our own legal class on our gallery. The guy who taught the class had obtained his Para-legal certificate from a correspondence course that he had to pay for. We took turns reading aloud from our cells and we would have homework assignments and quizzes. On Fridays we would have what became known as "free style-

Fridays," where each person would share something that they'd come across during the week. It could be a passage from a book, a piece of original poetry that someone had written, and some guys would rap as someone else in a cell close by would provide the beat. I was enjoying the process of learning and I began to read different books on religion, history, people, etc...

At one point, I took part in a Restorative Justice class that was given by DePaul University. I read books I never thought I'd read. Writings by Plato, Michelle Slexander, Socrates, Angela Davis, Cornell West, Aristotle, Paulo Freire, etc... It was during this time that I read a book called "Brainwashed" by Tom Bussell. It was a book about the power of images and how the things that we see constantly on a day to day basis (commercials, television shows, marketing ads, etc...) affect our subconscious. It caused me to do a survey throughout Stateville that was basically two questions: Between the ages of 13 and 19, what were your 3 favorite movies? Which actors were you drawn to? A overwhelming number of individuals stated the same 3 movies but in different order. "Menace to Society," "Boyz-N-The-Hood," and "Scarface." Now I'm not claiming that movies cause crime, but I am saying that images are a vital part of a developing mind when it comes to who we wish to become and how we want to define ourselves.

For me personally, I just wish that it didn't take me coming to prison for me to realize my own potential. Today, I continue to strive to become a better man, father, son, brother, and friend to others. I continue to hold fast to my relationship with God and pray that He continues to watch over my family and friends.

And last but not least, the guy that I wrote about earlier, Blue. Well, I ran across him during this bid and you know what? He's changed as well. We both speak about change, our families, freedom and a second chance. Talk about living and learning. I just hope that someone, anyone, who comes across this book will choose to learn from other peoples' experiences in this book versus learning from a negative life experience of their own. Prison is big business at it's finest and they've always got a bed open for you. But take it from me, in the words of the late, great Marvin Gaye "This Ain't Livin'"

***

__Jovon Scott, DOB 09-15-1988, Incarcerated 2009, Eligible Parole 2033, Aggravated Battery with a firearm and Aggravated Discharge of fireman.__

I'm 29 years old and have been incarcerated for 11 years. My family consisted of my mother, 9 sisters, and 1 brother. Since I've known, I've always gravitated towards the things that I was taught – violence, gangs, and no real sense of developing a moral compass. I joined the Black Disciples gang when I was 14 years old. I didn't have much of a connection with my natural family, and I was looking for acceptance.

Although I'm still an active of the Black Disciples, it doesn't define the man I am today, nor the man that I'm striving to be. All I've ever known was the struggle and being a part of a family in some fashion. When I was younger, it had been child service (DCFS) and now that I'm older, it's the department of corrections. Prison is where I found solace and true tranquility.

Is change needed? Most definitely. Someday I will leave the gang. But the main thing that keeps me involved isn't because I'm a high-ranking official, it's because this is the closet thing I have to a family. Perhaps someday I will become a successful author or a screen-play writer.

The worst uptake I can account for would be me joining the gang, but it's like I've done too much to move on and invested too much to look back. Life goes on for those who want it to, even while in prison. Determination is as good as a person who never sleeps.

***

A. D. AKA Tank, Aggravated battery with a firearm

I'm 27 years old and was raised in a Chicago suburb, Glennwood, with father, mother, and 1 younger sibling. I joined the Black Stone nation when I was age 17. I did not feel peer pressure to do so, Black Stone was in the area and I liked what they were doing and wanted to be a part of it. I made a conscious choice to become a gang member and have no regrets.

I enjoyed my early years in grade school and made good grades until reaching the 5th grade. This was when I began having major disciplinary problems and feeling depressed. By the 6th grade I believed that no one cared for me and that I would not be missed. At age 21 I began to see a purpose to my life when my daughter was born. Having a family and a good job is important to me when I am released, but I will not leave Black Stone.

***

A. H. Incarcerated for attempted murder.

I'm 26 years old and was raised in Humbolt Park, a community area on the West Side of Chicago. I have 2 siblings with me being the younger. My mother raised me while my father was in prison. I joined the Cobra Nation when I was 12 years old. There was not any peer pressure to join a gang. My brother came home from prison when I was 10 years old. I watched him and his friends who were all part of the Cobra Nation. They were gangbanging and doing a lot of violent acts. I saw all of the money they had with the nice cars and girls. I wanted that.

I'm not looking for change. The Cobra Nation is all that I know. There's something within me that does not want to let it go. I would not do violent acts to anyone outside of prison, but I would inside the prison. Inside I can act quicker and easier and I have to follow orders given to me.

If I were in prison for life, I would never leave the Cobra Nation. But if I was out and had a family, I might not be an active gang member.

Epilogue

While we have shared our experiences with gangs on the streets of Chicago and the path to a better life, it is our hope that you will avoid our mistakes. But to better prepare you for living on the streets, an awareness of basis information is helpful in navigating above, below, and around the obstacles you will face. And to be aware of the community support that reinforces what we have shared, and will keep you on the better path.

For decades there has been a tough-on-crime mentality that saw prison populations, together with the corresponding cost of prosecuting and housing offenders explode. The focus on diversion and rehabilitation programs normally backed by more liberal Democrats is now aligned with the historically conservative push to cut operating cost. One would like to think that the change is driven by our desire to improve humanity. But the reasons become clear when we look at Illinois' fiscal situation. Illinois has $15 billion of unpaid bills and a quarter-trillion dollars owed to public employees when they retire.

The Illinois Department of Juvenile Justice (IDJJ) was created in 2006 with a mission of enhancing public safety and positive youth outcomes by providing strength-based, individualized services to youth in a safe, learning and treatment environment so they might successfully reintegrate back into the community. Having said that, the Department has struggled to fulfill its mission. According to Acting Director Heidi Mueller, "We began as an under-resourced, ill-equipped agency attempting to serve the needs of Illinois' most troubled and vulnerable youth."

In 2012, the IDJJ was sued by the ACLU for not meeting the basic educational, mental health and safety needs of our youth. The following year led to the *MH v. Findley* lawsuit against the Prison Review Board for lack of due process in the parole revocation process. Both lawsuits were settled with the IDJJ, admitting failures and recognizing that we must do better.

But in 2016, there are reasons for optimism; a strategic operating guide; the Youth Assessment and Screening Instrument (YASI); CaseWorks assessment tool; and the opening of a Day Reporting Center in Chicago and a second Center in East St. Louis where youth on Aftercare can receive community-based reports. We overhauled our use of confinement; were found 100% compliant on our first full PREA audits; and achieved compliance by our federal monitor on the *MH v. Findley* remedial plan.

Whether or not a minor is placed in the Illinois juvenile justice system depends on several factors. When police pick up a youngster on the streets of Chicago for a possible criminal violation, the minor is asked for the name of his parents who are then notified that their child is being held at the local police station. If they are unable to contact the parents, a guardian, or the child's legal representative, an attorney assigned to represent the minor will be present. The age of the young person and the alleged crime will determine how long they can be held. In most situations the child will be released in the parents care. But if the act is more serious, a judge will be asked to intervene and determine if the child should be released or sent to the Juvenile Detention Center. The criminal act and the age of the offender will determine if the child is tried as a juvenile or an adult.

Current Illinois laws are intended to provide more flexibility in sentencing minors. The judge considers a number of factors, including a minor's age and cognitive ability, home life, degree of participation in a crime, criminal history and potential for rehabilitation. But judges can issue tougher sentences based on whether a gun was used or if the crime was committed against a police officer, corrections worker or paramedic.

If the youngster is found guilty and sentenced to prison, he is sent to the Juvenile Detention Center where he will be evaluated to determine which juvenile correction center he will spend his time, not to exceed age 21. If additional time is warranted, he will be sent to the Stateville Correctional Center where he will be interviewed, evaluated, and assigned to an Illinois prison for adults.

But it is our hope that the minor can be saved before crossing the red line, the path to a prison cell or death. A number of new laws are designed to keep more juveniles out of the prison system, including changes that stop minors from being detained for misdemeanor crimes and giving judges more discretion on whether teens should be tried as juveniles or adults. The mandatory life sentence for minors convicted of murder has been eliminated, and another recent law keeps children younger than 13 out of the justice system by placing them with community service providers instead of a juvenile detention facility. The objective is to reach those young people who are most able to improve through counseling and other programs instead of grouping them in with older teens at detention facilities.

While there are various community groups that help you, there is one in Chicago that supports our message throughout this book. It is here that you can join a family of like-minded young people led by concerned leaders like Father David Kelly, C.PP.S, offering promises of a better life.

At first glance you would think that David Kelly -- a middle-age, slender figure of a man -- is a long distant runner. But when you take a closer look, his smile and friendly eyes tell us there is more beyond the surface. Father David Kelly, C.PP.S., is the Executive Director of the Precious Blood Ministry of Reconciliation (PBMR), located in the Back of the Yards neighborhood, a hot-bed for Chicago gangs. The PBMR is a network of reconciliation ministries inspired by a spirituality of the Precious Blood; motivated by the belief that "those who were once far off have been brought near through the blood of Christ" (Eph. 2:13).

Like-minded priests and sisters had meetings over a two year period where they shared stories of the suffering they had witnessed and experienced, and their work for reconciliation. They held a unique curiosity over what it would be like to have a ministry whose sole purpose was to work for healing and understanding in the midst of violence and alienation in our world. Their ministry reached out to a community affected by violence in Chicago, and to the wider Church, offering a therapeutic process. Thus, the Precious Blood Ministry of Reconciliation was born in 2000.

The current home for the PBMR and the Second Chance Alternative High School is at 5114 S. Elizabeth Street. This building has become known as the Precious Blood Center, a safe place where people feel welcome and a sense of belonging. This is where relationships are built, a place to share our needs, hopes, and dreams.

Father Kelly is also the Cook County Jail and Cook County Juvenile Detention Center chaplain, and affiliated with the Kolbe House, an agency of the Department of Parish

Vitality and Mission of the Archdiocese of Chicago, dealing directly with those involved in the criminal justice system.

According to Jeff Herndon with FOX32 news, Father Kelly believes he knows how to make a difference. "I think certain things work, and I know things that are not working," Kelly says. "Our kids grow up knowing someone who has been killed. They know it's dangerous to walk from that door to that pool. You just gotta watch your back." We have young people who feel vulnerable, who are at risk, and feel like they have nobody backing them. You mix that with availability of guns, and you have young people who feel they need a gun to survive.

Breaking the cycle begins with us, Father Kelly says. We as adults need to communicate that we have your back, and that we care about you. From there, we focus on education and employment. And guns, we've got to get rid of them. We don't stop them with harsher laws. We stop the flow and the need so the 14 year old doesn't feel compelled to carry a gun. For this to work, Father Kelly says we must make it personal, even if we believe it's not our problem. "These are our kids, how would you feel if they were your kids?"

One can better appreciate the connections made between young people off the streets of Chicago and the PBMR by the writings on their website – pbmr.org The openness and caring in each story serves as a template for others searching for the family setting available through the Precious Blood Center. When you begin to share feelings, you will find a friend.

***

For the fifteen young men who gathered for a recent Making Choices Circle at the Precious Blood Center, it began as always, with a poem and a check-in. Fr. Kelly took us through a short meditation exercise, and then he proceeded to read us a fictional story about a boy named Raoul who was embarrassed in front of his friends by another boy who told the group that Raoul's mother was a crackhead. Most of our boys agreed that Raoul had no control of his mother's conduct, and that he shouldn't be ashamed or humiliated by her actions. As we passed the talking piece around the Circle, however, it became evident that for at least several of our young men, Raoul's story was also their story, and they understood his feelings completely.

First, it was Reggie's turn. He told the group that his mother was a crack head too, and that as he was growing up, he told his friends that his mother was dead. He couldn't live with the shame of having a mother who was a drug addict. Across the room, Wesley's face lit up. Wesley rarely says much in our Circles, but Reggie's comments hit home. His mother was also a crack head, and he too denied her existence to his friends, especially when he was young. Finally, Wayne, who was sitting next to me, told the group that the stories told by Reggie and Wesley rang true to him—he also lives with the shame of a drug addicted mother.

Wayne's hurt was in evidence earlier in the day. I went to pick Wayne up at his sister's house where he occasionally flops because his father and mother do not have jobs or a stable place to live. I've met Wayne's Dad on a couple of occasions, but I've never met his mother, and Wayne has only spoken of her twice in the fours years I've mentored him. She has been addicted to drugs his entire life. To my surprise, Wayne mentioned that his mother was upstairs and that they were waiting for an ambulance to take her to the hospital. I asked Wayne if I could go up to meet her, and Wayne said, "You don't want to meet her." When I protested that I really would like to meet her, Wayne repeated, emphatically this time, "You don't want to meet her!"

My childhood experiences are far removed from the trauma experienced by these young men. Yes, I went through a period where I was embarrassed by my parents. I didn't think my father was as "cool" as my friends' fathers — he was an undertaker, and I took a lot of ribbing for that. Pretty trivial stuff when compared to the family dysfunction, poverty, pain, and violence these youth live with everyday.

During our Circles and at our Center, we try to create safe places where our young men and women can tell their stories in an environment where respect, honesty, confidentially, and listening is valued. For at least three of the young men in this Circle, they also found out they are not alone.

***

"He wasn't a bad kid. I mean, he wasn't perfect, but he was a good kid. He didn't deserve to die like that." It was if he had to defend his son even in death. Too many people had questioned why his son was killed. "Was he into something? Was he in a gang? What was he doing that he got killed?" Too often families tell of how they feel as though they have to defend their loved ones even when they are the victims of a horrific crime.

Late Sunday afternoon, as I was saying goodbye to our Hope and Healing group – a support group for families who have lost a loved one to violence – I received a call to ask me to come to the hospital. "Father, can you come to the hospital? Andy was shot; they say he won't make it." I arrived at the hospital, celebrated the sacrament of the sick, and anointed Andy, but his wound was too grave and his heart gave out.

Only a week before his death, after mass, on the steps of the church, Andy spoke to me about enrolling into college. He had graduated some months before and was working at McDonalds. He wanted more out of his life. He wanted something that would give him a future. As he left, he turned and embraced me and said he'd call. Andy had just turned eighteen years old.

One of the things that families who have lost a child to violence always say is that many people presume that their son, somehow, brought the violence on to themselves. As we were planning the funeral, in the midst of his grief, Andy's father spoke of his kid who struggled, but was simply in the wrong place at the wrong time. He was killed in the middle of the afternoon on a Sunday. He was with his friends, riding in a car – nothing more. He was a victim of violence.

Andy's older brother only recently returned from Iraq after his tour of duty. He returned back home to Chicago after his four years with the US Army were completed. It is ironic, if not tragic, that he comes back from war to the death of his little brother on the streets of Chicago.

One might be tempted to see this as an urban issue, as something that is confined to the streets of places like Chicago. But school bullying, drug dependency, and family and institutional dysfunction is not limited to urban America. One only need to pick up the newspaper or turn on the television to hear stories of how violence has interrupted and changed forever the lives of yet another family, another community.

I cannot tell you how many community gatherings, town hall meetings, and strategy sessions I have participated in an attempt to address the violence among our youth. The question as to why there is so much violence, drug abuse, and polarization within our communities seems to be the topic of many agenda. Why do so many youth seemingly have so little direction in their lives? Why is there so much violence in families and communities? Why are kids killing kids? What can we do?

While so many are focusing on stricter laws and harsher punishment, the church is called upon to do what she does best – to reach out and heal. Programs addressed, not to punish, but heal those who are caught up in violence seems to be more in line with who we are as a community of believers.

The first step toward learning how to prevent any health problem, and violence is a health problem, is to discover what causes it. Once we know what causes it, we know a bit more about how we are to overcome it, neutralize it, or remove it. Violence, as opposed to some of the other health issues, is caused by humanity.

"Hurt people hurt people", says Carl Bell, a noted psychologist. If we are to overcome violence that plagues our communities and families, we must work to attend to those who carry so much pain and hurt. As a church, we can begin by reaching out and working toward healing and reconciliation. Providing the space and time to allow someone to voice their pain and connect with themselves and others is one way in which we can reduce the violence that is too often the result of feeling isolated and alienated. Violence causes, and is a result of the alienation and the loss of connectedness with those around us.

It is not that our work ends with building relationships, but it has to begin there. All the programs and intervention strategies cannot take the place of building and sustaining relationships with those who feel isolated from the world around them. A victim of violence or trauma feels as though they are alone. Whether it be the young person who is a victim of bullying, our men and women coming back from war, or the young person on the streets of Chicago, the stories are of feeling numb, or of feeling they don't belong, of trying anything to bring feeling back into their lives are told.

The Precious Blood Ministry of Reconciliation is a ministry of the Missionaries of the Precious Blood charged to work toward healing and reconciliation in and among the communities in which we live and in our Church communities. We have embraced many means to gather people together and create spaces – sacred spaces – where stories are told and relationships can be built or repaired. Some of those methods, such as the peacemaking circle, are teachable and usable in a host of situations. As we strive to be relevant and aware of the "ever changing times" let us reach out to those within our communities who are estranged or in pain and make a place for them – a place of hospitality and care.

The parish church/school continues to be a safe haven in our communities. For many, it is a place of trust and acceptance. We must embrace the unique gift given us through the blood of Jesus; we must embrace the ministry of reconciliation, not as an afterthought, but as the very core of who we are. We have the special gift and honor to tread in places where others cannot tread. We are called to allow the stories to be told and to honor those stories in how we live.

***

When asked about his 25 years as the prison chaplain at the Menard maximum-security prison in Chester, Illinois, Father Leo J. Hayes was asked if he talked with incarcerated gang members about their crimes. (Father Hayes is currently retired and writing his memoir.) Perhaps his answer was a blueprint for reaching out to those who traveled the path of destruction, but look for a better way. "The best policy is to never ask about an inmate's history. Speak of it only if he brings it up. The barrier in prisons is the inmate's terrible history. Who could love that history? So, the chaplain, who else, must look beyond that history to the child of God, Heir of Heaven, precious human being that lies hidden; that no administrator, no counselor is going to see. Guilt does not wipe out their underlying goodness as a human being. The most important thing for an inmate to learn is that he is loved so he can see that he is lovable, and therefore love himself."

Hayes went on to explain, "Love, unconditional positive regard, is conveyed to the inmate through the eyes, and that the chaplain must find the balance between staring and looking away. A gentle look into their soul, through their eyes, is the pathway for the inmate to see that he is valued. This happens through listening, questioning, and seeing."

Be mindful of prisoners as if sharing their imprisonment,
and of the ill-treated as of yourselves, for you also are in the body.
Hebrews 13:3

Glossary

Baddest – Mean, tough, hard, not afraid, and sometimes mean crazy.

Bling – Wearing a lot of shinny jewelry.

Blunt – When you remove the inside of a cigar and replace it with marijuana.

Brick – Another word for a kilo of cocaine.

Broad – Another name for a girl or woman.

Cannon – Hang gun.

Chief – The leader of a gang.

Cop – To cop is to buy drugs.

Crack – Cocaine when it is in rock form.

Crib – Another name for your home.

Cush – High quality marijuana.

Desert Eagle – The brand name for a particular gun.

Dropped – When you are killed.

Dumping – *Shooting.*

Flip – When you buy drugs and sell them for a profit.

Freak – A person having sex, or doing anything while having sex.

Homies – Another word for friend.

Jocking – When you overly like someone because of what they have.

Lame – A name for someone that you don't think is cool.

Mean Mugging – When you walk around with your faced masked up trying to scare people.

Merked – To be badly beaten or killed.

Opposition – *Gangs refer to other gangs as the opposition*

Original Gangster – *O.G.* *Someone who has been a gangster for 25 years.*

Pissy – Has many meanings, but in this book it is used to describe a hallway where people urinate. Can also be used for someone who is dirty.

Popped – You were shot or arrested.

Poppin' Pills – People are popping drugs in the form of pills.

Ride/Ride – Can mean car, cars, friend, or friends.

Stang – Can be used to describe someone who is a target, or someone you trick out of something.

Shorties – Can be used to describe young kids in the streets or your girl.

Swag – Means you are cool or you show high self-confidence.

Sucker – A person who does not have the swag or street smarts.

Tella Tale – Name given to someone who is a snitch.

The bug crew – Drug addicted inmates in a prison.

Trickin' off – When you spend your money.

Wanna Be's – Someone who wants to be in the streets, but just doesn't have it.

Whip – A car.